THE BOY ALLIES IN THE BALKAN CAMPAIGN

OR, The Struggle to Save a Nation

CLAIR W. HAYES

1ˢᵗ WORLD LIBRARY Literary Society

The Boy Allies in the Balkan Campaign

Clair W. Hayes

© 1st World Library, 2009
PO Box 2211
Fairfield, IA 52556
www.1stworldlibrary.com
First Edition

LCCN: 2009923369

Softcover ISBN: 978-1-4218-8821-7
Hardcover ISBN: 978-1-4218-8920-7
eBook ISBN: 978-1-4218-8722-7

Purchase *"The Boy Allies in the Balkan Campaign"*
as a traditional bound book at:
www.1stWorldLibrary.com/purchase.asp?ISBN=978-1-4218-8821-7

1st World Library is a literary, educational organization
dedicated to:

- Creating a free internet library of downloadable ebooks

- Hosting writing competitions and offering book publishing
scholarships.

1st World Library Literary Society

Giving Back to the World

"If you want to work on the core problem, it's early school literacy."

- James Barksdale, former CEO of Netscape

"No skill is more crucial to the future of a child, or to a democratic and prosperous society, than literacy."

- Los Angeles Times

"Literacy... means far more than learning how to read and write... The aim is to transmit... knowledge and promote social participation."

- UNESCO

"Literacy is not a luxury, it is a right and a responsibility. If our world is to meet the challenges of the twenty-first century we must harness the energy and creativity of all our citizens."

- President Bill Clinton

"Parents should be encouraged to read to their children, and teachers should be equipped with all available techniques for teaching literacy, so the varying needs and capacities of individual kids can be taken into account."

- Hugh Mackay

CONTENTS

CHAPTER I

IN THE AIR

"And how do you feel now, Mr. Stubbs?"

Hal Paine took his eyes from the distance ahead long enough to gaze toward that part of the military aeroplane in which three other figures were seated. It might rather be said, however, that two of the others were seated, for the third figure was huddled up in a little ball, now and then emitting feeble sounds.

In response to Hal's question, this huddled figure straight-tened itself up long enough to make reply.

"I feel sick," came the answer in a low voice. "How long before we can get back to earth, so that I may die peacefully?"

"Oh, I guess you won't die, Mr. Stubbs," said Hal, chuckling a bit to himself.

He turned his eyes ahead again and gave his entire attention to guiding the swiftly flying craft.

The first streak of dawn had appeared in the east but a few moments before and gradually now it was growing light.

High in the air, it was very chilly and those in the aeroplane had drawn their coats closely about them.

"Where do you suppose we are now, Hal?"

This speaker was another of the passengers in the car, Chester Crawford, chum and bosom companion of Hal.

"Somewhere over Central Austria," replied Hal, not taking his eyes from ahead.

"I would rather that it were over Serbia, Montenegro or Greece," said the fourth occupant of the airship, Colonel Harry Anderson of His British Majesty's service. "I'm beginning to get a little cramped up here. I'd like to stretch my legs a bit."

"You won't ever stretch them again, you may be sure of that," said a hollow voice, none other than that of Anthony Stubbs, American war correspondent, who now aroused himself enough to predict dire results.

"What?" said Colonel Anderson. "And why won't I ever stretch my legs again?"

"The undertaker'll do it for you," groaned Stubbs. "This contraption is bound to come down pretty quick and when it does it'll be all off."

"Can't see why that should worry you any," remarked the colonel cheerfully. "It won't be your funeral."

"No, but I'll have one at about the same time," Stubbs moaned. "I go down when you do."

He raised his voice a trifle. "Let's go down, Hal," he

continued. "I'm awfully sick."

"Go down nothing," ejaculated Chester. "Think we want to give the Austrians another chance at us, huh?"

"Better be shot by an Austrian than to die in this infernal machine," declared Stubbs in a feeble voice.

"This," said Chester calmly, "is an airship and not an infernal machine."

"Well, it's my idea of an infernal machine, all the same," Stubbs groaned. "We'll all come down in pieces, as sure as you're a foot high."

"Oh, I guess not," said Chester. "We—whoa, there."

He broke off suddenly and seized the side of the machine, as did Colonel Anderson, just as the craft tilted dangerously to one side.

"Help!" came a cry from Stubbs, as he went rolling toward the side of the craft.

There appeared to be no danger that the little man would be thrown out, for the sides of the basket-like craft protected him, but he was plainly frightened and Chester gave him a hand, now that the machine had righted itself again.

"It's all right, Stubbs," the lad said; "no danger at all. Sit up, now."

The little man shook off the hand.

"I don't want to sit up," he whimpered. "I want to jump overboard and end all this suspense. I might as well die now as ten minutes from now. Oh my, I wish—"

"Well, Mr. Stubbs," came Hal's voice, "unless I miss my guess, you are likely to get your wish. Here comes one of the enemy to watch you die."

"What's that?" exclaimed Chester and Colonel Anderson in a single voice.

"Off to the right," replied Hal, quietly.

Glancing in that direction, Chester and Colonel Anderson saw a large air craft headed in their direction.

"After us, do you think?" asked Chester.

"Can't tell," replied Hal, briefly.

"Hardly probable," said Colonel Anderson. "Chances are the fellow believes we are one of his own kind and wants a word with us."

"Maybe you're right," said Hal. "I'll hold to my present course anyhow and take a chance."

The aeroplane continued on as before.

Now Stubbs came to life once more.

"Well, why don't you get a little speed out of this thing?" he demanded. "What are you going to do? Stand right here and let that fellow get us? What's the matter with you, anyhow? Trying to get me killed?"

"Why, Mr. Stubbs," exclaimed Chester, in mock seriousness, "I thought that you were simply dying to be killed. Here's an

Clair W. Hayes

Austrian coming in direct answer to your prayers. What's the difference whether he gets you now or ten minutes from now? It'll be all the same in a hundred years."

"Think you're smart, don't you," snapped Stubbs. "Why should I want to be killed? I ask you now, why should I want to be killed?"

"Well, really, I don't know," replied Chester, "unless it is because you are so awfully sick."

"Sick!" shouted Stubbs. "Sick! Who said anything about being sick?"

"Why, I understood you to say—"

"Well, you understood wrong. Sick? No, I'm not sick, but we'll all be worse than sick if Hal can't coax a little speed out of this machine. Say!" this to Hal, "what are you waiting for, anyhow?"

"Now you just hold your horses, Stubbs," replied Hal. "I'm running this party at this moment and I'm going to run it my own way. Colonel Anderson, if you hear any more out of our war-corresponding friend, kindly sit on him, will you?"

"With pleasure," replied the colonel briefly.

"Oh, you will, will you?" cried Stubbs. "Well, you won't. I—I'll—"

He subsided after muttering to himself for some moments.

The others now gave their undivided attention to the other craft, which by this time had drawn close to them.

"Man wig-wagging forward, Hal," said Chester.

"I see him," replied Hal, "but I can't make out his signals. Can you, Anderson?"

"No, I can't. He evidently has something to say, though."

"Well," said Hal, "we'll have to hold a sudden council of war. What are we going to do about it? Shall we stop and talk, trying to fool him, or shall we run for it?"

"Well, if we were going to run, it would have been better before he got so close," said Chester. "Guess we may as well see what he has to say. These Austrian uniforms won't come in bad. You do the talking, Hal."

Hal nodded.

"All right," he said.

He reduced the speed of the machine and the Austrian came closer.

"Ahoy, there!" he said in German. "Who are you?"

"Lieutenant Drizladaz, attached to the Austrian army at Trieste," Hal shouted back.

"What are you doing here?"

"Mission," Hal yelled.

"Where to?"

Hal thought quickly.

"Greece," he said finally.

"What for?"

"That," said Hal, "is none of your business. I have my orders and I haven't time to fool around here with you. I'm due back to-morrow night."

There was a moment's silence from the other machine and then a voice called:

"Has your mission anything to do with Greece's intervention in the war?"

"Well, I can't say anything about that," replied the lad, thinking to give the other the impression that it was.

"I see," was the answer shouted back. "Well, I wish you luck. Sorry you can't tell me all about it."

"You probably will know soon enough," replied Hal.

"Good. Don't want any company, do you?"

"No, I guess not."

"You want to be careful crossing the Balkans. I understand there are some British and French aircraft with the Serbians and Montenegrins. Look out for them."

"I'll be on guard," replied Hal. "Thanks for the information."

"Tell you what," said the Austrian, "I've been doing some scout duty there myself. I'll just trail along. May be able to help you out a bit"

Hal didn't think much of this plan.

"I can make it all right myself," he declared.

"Suppose you can," was the reply, "but it is just as well to be on the safe side."

"Well, suit yourself," said Hal, "but don't expect me to wait for you."

"If you can distance me you will have to travel," returned the Austrian. "I've the fastest craft in the service."

"I'm glad to hear that," replied Hal, and added to himself: "I don't think."

"Set your pace," continued the Austrian. "I'll trail along behind."

"No use talking any more, I guess," Hal muttered to his friends. "May as well go along."

Chester and Colonel Anderson nodded their assent and the machine moved forward again.

Things might have gone well had it not been for Stubbs. Suddenly the little man uttered a yell and sat up straight in his seat.

"Ouch!" he shouted. "I've got an awful pain!"

Clair W. Hayes

CHAPTER II

MONTENEGRIN MOUNTAINEERS

Hal drew a sharp breath and tightened his hold upon the steering wheel.

There was no question that Stubbs' voice had carried to the occupants of the second craft, and as Stubbs had exclaimed aloud in English there was little doubt in the minds of our three friends that the Austrians would seek an explanation. Nor were they wrong.

Came a hail from the Austrian:

"Who've you got aboard, there?"

"Prisoner," replied Hal, thinking quickly.

"What are you doing with him?"

"We—" Hal began, but the Austrian interrupted.

"Spies, that's what you are! Down to the ground now, or I'll put a hole through you."

"Guess it's no use fooling any longer," muttered Hal.

He threw over the elevating lever and the large craft soared rapidly. At the same moment a shot rang out from aboard the Austrian, followed by a cry of surprise, and then the Austrian gave chase.

"Get your guns and see if you can pick 'em off," Hal instructed Chester and Colonel Anderson. "I'll run this thing, but you fellows will have to do the fighting."

"Suits me," responded Chester, examining his revolver carefully.

Colonel Anderson also nodded his agreement to this plan.

Hal now changed his course and the airship headed toward the south, bearing off a trifle to the east, in a direction that he believed, eventually, would land them in Serbia.

It became apparent now that the Austrian had not boasted of the speed of his craft without reason, for he gained perceptibly.

"We can't out-run him, Hal," shouted Chester.

"Then we shall have to try something else," was the reply.

Abruptly he reduced the speed of the craft and the Austrians dashed in range of the revolvers of the fugitives almost before they could have realized it.

"Crack! Crack!"

Chester and Colonel Anderson had fired. There came a scream of pain from behind and the Austrian craft wobbled crazily. A moment later a man sprang to his feet, sought to retain his footing, threw up his arms and went hurtling into space.

"Got one, Hal!" said Chester, quietly.

"Good!"

Came a volley of small arm fire from behind and bullets whined about the four friends. Again Chester and Colonel Anderson fired almost simultaneously and again their efforts were rewarded. A second man was put out of the fight, as they could see.

At this moment Stubbs came into action.

He arose from his seat and, grasping the side of the speeding craft with his left hand for support, stood to his full height. His right arm drew back, then flashed sharply forward again and a small object went spinning through the air toward the Austrian airship.

It struck home and there was a terrible explosion, followed by several sharp cries of pain, as the Austrian airship seemed to split into a thousand pieces. A moment later these pieces disappeared.

The three friends turned upon Stubbs.

"What is this, magic?" asked Chester in surprise.

"No," replied Stubbs, quietly. "Melenite. I just happened to see a stick of it here, so I threw it."

"Well, you did a pretty good job, Stubbs," said Colonel Anderson.

"I didn't pitch for my college team two years for nothing,"

returned Stubbs modestly. "But now let's go down. I want to get my feet on the ground again."

"It won't be much longer, Stubbs," said Hal. "Another two hours at this speed should put us across the Serbian frontier. Just be patient."

"I'll wait," replied Stubbs, "but I won't promise to be patient."

He sank back to his place and refused to talk further.

While the big army craft is speeding across Austria it will be a good time to explain the presence of the four friends in their present predicament and introduce them briefly to those who have not met them before.

Hal Paine and Chester Crawford were both American lads. With the former's mother, they had been in Berlin at the outbreak of the great war, and, after a series of interesting and exciting adventures, they made their way to Liege just in time to take part in the defense of that stronghold with the Belgian army.

There they won distinction and lieutenancies in the Belgian service, the latter bestowed upon them by King Albert himself. They had been in France with the British troops that had stopped the German drive on Paris and had gone with the Allied army on its advance. They had seen service on all fronts and now considered themselves veteran campaigners.

Colonel Anderson they had met in Berlin just after the Kaiser had declared war upon France. The colonel, lieutenant then, and Major Derevaux, a Frenchman, had taken the boys with them on their flight and the four had later encountered each other in many strange and unexpected places.

Clair W. Hayes

Stubbs they also had met while on one of their many missions and had earned the little man's undying gratitude; but he had repaid whatever they had done for him, with interest, more than once.

The boys, in their latest exploit, had been with the Italian army in the Alps. Two of the four friends having fallen into the hands of the enemy, the others had entered the enemy's lines in an effort to effect their escape.

It was a daring adventure, but after a fight and chase, the four had managed to seize the airship in which we now find them and had at last fought their way clear. They had then held a council of war and decided that it was best to head for the Balkans, rather than to run the gauntlet of the Austrian flying craft which kept constant vigil in the direction of the Italian lines.

Hal and Chester, typical American lads, were large and strong for their ages, which were within a year of each other, seventeen and eighteen now. In the rough lumber camps of the north, the two had had considerable experience in the use of firearms and the art of self-defense—fists. Also, during the school term each had practiced the use of the sword until, though by no means experts, they could give a fair account of themselves with this weapon—as each had done more than once.

Fortunately, both lads had made a study of languages and spoke French and German fluently. They never had trouble on that score.

The great war up to this point had not gone as successfully as the Entente Allies had hoped in the early days. The German lines on all fronts were seemingly stronger than ever before. Even the entrance of Italy into the war on the side of the

Allies had failed to turn the balance, as it had been confidently expected it would. East and west, the German lines held, while in the Balkans the enemy was even now advancing against the heroic little Serbian army, which, before many days, was to be forced to relinquish its country to the iron heel of the invader. Montenegro, the smallest factor in the war, still was fighting hard—the rugged and gigantic mountaineers giving a good account of themselves upon all sides.

This was the situation, then, as the airship containing Colonel Anderson, British officer, Anthony Stubbs, American war correspondent, and Hal Paine and Chester Crawford sped southward over Austria.

Several hours after the sinking of the Austrian aeroplane Chester spoke.

"Where do you suppose we are now, Hal?" he asked.

"I believe we must have crossed the frontier," replied Hal. "However, we'll wait another half hour before descending to have a look."

The half hour up, Hal sent the airship lower and lower. Soon, a faint gray speck below became visible, assuming larger and larger proportions, until all aboard made out the ground beneath.

And then, half a mile ahead, a body of troops were seen. Hal checked the speed of the craft immediately.

"Don't know who they are," he explained. "We'll be careful. They may be all right and then again they may not be."

He sent the machine higher again and a few minutes later the craft hung directly above the troops below.

"I can't make out those uniforms," declared Chester.

"Nor I," said Hal. "However, they are not Austrian, I can see that. We'll take a chance and go down."

Again the machine moved closer toward the earth, and a few minutes later came to rest upon the ground a short distance from the main body of troops. A squad of men, let by an officer, came hurriedly forward, covering the four friends with their rifles.

"By Jove!" exclaimed Colonel Anderson. "You must have miscalculated a bit, Hal. I recognize them now."

"Well, who are they?" demanded the lad.

"Montenegrins."

"Good," cried Chester. "Then we are among friends."

The four friends raised their hands in token of surrender as the officer and his men came toward them. A few paces away, the officer halted and addressed them.

Hal shook his head.

"Can't understand that lingo," he exclaimed.

He addressed the officer in English and the officer also indicated that he could not understand.

"Don't want to tackle him in German if I can help it," said Hal. "It might not suit him."

"Well, what's the matter with French?" Chester wanted to know.

"Nothing, I guess," returned Hal. "I'll try him. We are British officers," he said, addressing the Montenegrin officer, "and we have just escaped from the Austrians."

The Montenegrin understood and replied in broken French:

"How am I to know you are not of the enemy?"

"Well, I don't know, to tell the truth," Hal replied with a pleasant smile. "I am afraid it does look a little bad for us, as we have nothing to prove our identities. But if you have a British or French officer about here, perhaps we can convince him."

The Montenegrin nodded.

"Fortunately, we have," he said. He ordered one of his men to summon Colonel Edwards.

"By Jove!" said Anderson. "I know an Edwards. I wonder can it be the same?"

"No such luck, I am afraid," said Chester.

But it was; and a few moments later Colonel Edwards and Colonel Anderson were shaking hands affectionately.

Clair W. Hayes

CHAPTER III

THE KING OF THE MONTENEGRINS

With his hand upon Edwards' arm, Colonel Anderson approached Hal and Chester.

"I want you to meet my two young friends," he said.

Colonel Edwards shook hands with each lad in turn and then turned to Stubbs, who, during all this time, had been standing quietly, while he cast a critical eye upon the Montenegrin troopers who stood near.

"A likely looking bunch of men," he muttered to himself. "I'll bet they could give a good account of themselves in a—'

He faced about just in time to acknowledge Colonel Anderson's introduction to Colonel Edwards; then turned again to survey the mountaineers.

"Good fighters, these," he said to himself, "or I miss my guess."

"Now," said Hal to Colonel Edwards, "there is really no use of our standing here. I'd like to look up a place where I can turn in for a few winks. I'm dead tired and I imagine the rest of you are, too."

Chester seconded Hal's motion and Colonel Anderson admitted his own fatigue. Stubbs settled the matter.

"Where there are men there are beds," he said; "or at least cots, or pallets, or something. I'm going to find one."

He moved toward a row of tents in the distance.

"Hold on there," said Chester. "We're all going, Stubbs."

In the meantime Colonel Edwards had been holding a consultation with the Montenegrin officer who had first accosted the friends.

"I am sure that if you vouch for them they are all right," said the Montenegrin.

"Thanks," said Edwards. "Then, with your permission, I shall conduct them to my own quarters."

"And you may also make free with mine," said the other.

Again Colonel Edwards expressed his thanks, in which the others joined, and then he led the way toward the distant tents.

Fifteen minutes later the four friends were sleeping soundly, with never a care in the world, for it had been long since they had closed their eyes and they were completely worn out.

Darkness shrouded the small tent when Hal opened his eyes. It was several moments before the lad could gain his bearings, but when at last he realized just where he was he bethought himself of the others.

Clair W. Hayes

"Still sleeping, I guess," he said.

He arose, moved to the door of the tent and passed out. A steady rumbling sound fell upon his ears and Hal, momentarily, was unable to account for it. But the solution soon came to him.

"Troops moving," he told himself.

He was right. Walking some distance from the tent, he made out, probably half a mile away, the dark forms of many men as they marched swiftly on in the darkness, their figures lighted up ever and anon by the gleam of a flashlight. But the camp in which the lad stood was perfectly quiet.

"Now I wonder—" he muttered—gazed silently ahead a moment and then turned back toward the tent, saying to himself: "Guess I'll wake the others up."

Chester and Colonel Anderson were aroused without much trouble. Not so Stubbs.

"What's the matter?" came the little man's query, when Hal prodded him gently in the ribs with his foot.

"Time to get up," said Hal, briefly.

For a moment Stubbs opened his eyes and peered into the darkness—for Hal had made no light.

"Get up?" he exclaimed. "What! Anthony Stubbs get up in the middle of the night? Not much!"

"But we are going, Stubbs," said Hal. "We don't want to leave you here by yourself."

"Kind of you," said Stubbs sarcastically. "I can remember when you were not so solicitious of my welfare. Don't worry about me. I'll just sleep right along."

He turned over and a loud snore a few moments later told that he was again in the land of dreams.

Again Hal prodded him with his foot.

"Stubbs! I say, Stubbs!" he called.

Directly Stubbs opened his eyes.

"And what's the matter this time?" he demanded aggrievedly.

"Hurry!" Hal exclaimed, thinking to get the little man up by a ruse. "The Austrians are coming."

"Run, then!" replied Stubbs. "I'll hide here. They won't bother me."

"Now listen here, Stubs," said Chester, "just when do you want to get up?"

Again Stubbs allowed his eyes to open and he peered into the darkness sleepily.

"What day is this?" he inquired mildly.

"Tuesday," replied Chester; "but what—"

"Then call me Saturday," said the little man gently, and closed his eyes in sleep once more.

"Ha! Ha!" laughed Colonel Anderson. "He had you there, Chester."

Chester appeared somewhat flustered.

"Well, he'll have to get up out of there," he said wrathfully.

"Oh, come on and let him be, Chester," said Hal. "I guess nothing will hurt him. We'll be back by daylight and I'll venture to say we will find him here, still snoring."

"Well, all right," Chester agreed at length; "but to tell you the truth, I don't just like that answer he gave me."

The three left the tent and Hal led the way toward where he had so recently perceived the passing troops.

Infantry, cavalry and artillery were still passing in dense masses, moving westward.

"I wonder where they are going?" said Chester.

"To the front, I suppose," replied Hal.

"Now do you really suppose they are?" asked Chester sarcastically. "I thought perhaps they were on dress parade. Say, just where are we anyhow? Do either of you know?"

"By Jove!" exclaimed Colonel Anderson. "I meant to ask Edwards, but I forgot all about it. He told us, you remember, he would be in the tent on our left. We'll go back and have him out. Perhaps we can learn a few things."

"Suits me," Hal agreed. "We can't see anything here but troops, and we have seen too many of them to be much interested. Come on."

Fifteen minutes later found them seated in the tent Colonel Edwards had commandeered for his temporary headquarters and the colonel himself doing the talking.

"You are perhaps fifteen miles northwest of Cettinje, the capital of Montenegro," he explained.

"And where are these troops going?" asked Hal.

"Reinforcements to the Austrian front," said Colonel Edwards. "Also some of them, can they be spared, will be rushed to the aid of the Serbians, who, from all accounts, are being sorely pressed by the new German offensive."

"New German offensive?" exclaimed Hal.

"Why, yes. Haven't you heard of it?"

"No. Will you explain?"

"I'll try," said Colonel Edwards. "I'll revert back to the start. On Friday, August 13, news reached London, where I was then stationed, that an Austro-German army of more than 300,000 men was massing at a point on the Serbian frontier and it was asserted that the Kaiser was about to strike a blow at Serbia in order to improve Teuton prospects in the Balkans, where Roumania and Greece had been reported as waiting a favorable opportunity to join the Allies.

"The great German victories in Russia, following the fall of Warsaw, had, however, caused the Balkan kingdoms to waver, and Bulgaria was said to have strong pro-German leanings. On August 16 the Austro-German army crossed the frontier and began a bombardment of Belgrade, the capital. This led to a crisis in the Greek parliament, where the Venizelos party caused the downfall of the cabinet, which supported the king's attitude of strict neutrality—a neutrality he had promised his consort, who is the sister of the Kaiser,

Clair W. Hayes

as you know.

"On August 21 Serbia made it known that in accordance with the advice of the Allies, she was willing to grant the demands of Bulgaria for the return of territory taken in the last Balkan war, and for a time it seemed that Bulgaria would enter the war on the side of the Allies. However, on September 19 it was said that Bulgaria would join the Central Powers, thus permitting Germany to establish an unbroken line of allies from the Baltic to the Bosporus.

"On October 5, the Allies, upon invitation of the Greek premier, began the disembarkation of troops at Saloniki to go to the assistance of the Serbians; and, so far as I know, they are still landing."

The three friends had listened attentively to this account of the Balkan situation. They had heard some inkling of the seriousness of the Serbian plight, but had not realized until now that Germany had at last set out to crush the little Balkan kingdom as she had crushed Belgium in the early days of the great war.

"And what is the latest on the Bulgarian attitude?" asked Colonel Anderson.

"Well, I haven't heard anything later than I have told you, but my personal opinion is that Bulgaria, sooner or later, will join the Germans."

"Fools," said Colonel Anderson, briefly.

"And Greece?" inquired Chester.

"I don't know, but I believe Greece will keep out of the war just as long as she possibly can. Certainly, the Greek people will never consent to aiding the Germans."

"You never can tell," said Colonel Anderson sententiously.

Outside the tent it was now growing light, for time had passed swiftly. Hal noticed the light filtering in.

"Great Scott! I had no idea it was morning," he said. "It must have been after midnight when we awoke. Let's get outside."

They left the tent and Hal went into their own quarters a moment, where he found Stubbs up and about to emerge. Together the five walked toward the eastern extremity of the camp.

Came a sudden blaring of trumpets and a body of horse swept toward them. The riders drew rein almost before the friends, dismounted and stood at attention, while a figure who had been in the center also jumped to the ground. This figure of huge stature, a man of advanced age, who dismounted nimbly in spite of his years, walked toward the spot where stood the five friends. Edwards came to attention, as did the others.

"The king!" said Colonel Edwards in a low voice.

Clair W. Hayes

CHAPTER IV

INTO THE MOUNTAINS

Nicholas, king of the Montenegrins, came forward slowly, his head bowed as though in grief, and it seemed for a moment as though he would pass Hal, Chester and the others without seeing them. But even as he drew abreast of the five, he looked up suddenly. His gaze rested upon Colonel Edwards and the Englishman bowed low. Colonel Anderson did likewise. Hal, Chester and Stubbs remained erect.

The king smiled slightly at Colonel Edwards, whom he plainly knew, and glanced inquiringly at the others.

Colonel Edwards approached him.

"Your majesty," he said, "I would crave your permission to present another of my countrymen and three Americans, who have seen service with your allies in the western theater of war."

The king nodded his head affirmatively and Colonel Edwards motioned the others to approach. The king extended a hand to each and spoke a few pleasant words.

"I hope," he said, "that you will make yourselves perfectly at home in my camp. I am sorry I have no better to offer you." He turned to Edwards. "I have faith in you English," he said, "and for that reason I was about to summon you this morning. I have a mission of importance, and some danger, I would have you undertake."

"I shall be pleased, sire" replied Colonel Edwards with a bow.

The king smiled.

"I knew you would be," he said. "Now this mission will necessitate probably more than a single man. You shall pick the others. It seems simple, but I can assure you it is not. Among the Albanian tribesmen, I am told, there is a disposition to doubt the justice of our cause and the cause of our allies. A spirit of unrest is rife there. I would have it looked into. I have faith in the majority of the Albanians, but a few agitators could do much harm right now. The reason I say one man could hardly undertake the task is that he would hardly have time to cover the necessary ground. Two might do; even more would be better."

At this point Colonel Anderson stepped forward.

"If you please, your majesty," he said, and hesitated.

"Speak, sir," said the king.

"If you please, your majesty," Colonel Anderson repeated, "it would give me, and my friends here, the utmost pleasure to be of some slight service to you. With your permission, we shall offer our services to Colonel Edwards."

A smile stole over the king's rugged face.

Clair W. Hayes

"I have always said," he declared, "that the British and the Americans come nearer to being like my own people than any others. You have my permission, sir, for yourself and your friends, and I have no doubt of the success of the mission." He turned again to Colonel Edwards. "You will make all possible haste?"

"What we may, with caution," was the reply.

"Good. Then I shall expect you back within the week."

Again all bowed before the king and after a few words of farewell the Montenegrin monarch resumed his walk.

"Well, I feel better now," declared Hal. "We've got something to do, so we won't feel as though we had no business here."

"My sentiments, exactly," agreed Chester.

"Well, they are not mine," declared Stubbs. "Say! what's the matter with you fellows, anyhow? Look at all the trouble we had finding a safe place to come down, and now you are running around looking for more trouble. You are not going to get Anthony Stubbs into any Albanian mountains, I can tell you that."

"You don't have to go if you don't want to, I'm sure," said Colonel Anderson stiffly. "I had no idea you were afraid."

"Afraid!" echoed Stubbs. "And why shouldn't I be afraid, I ask you? Why shouldn't I be afraid, eh? I don't know anything about mountains. I don't know anything about mountaineers. I don't want to know anything about any of them. All I want to do is—"

"Get a little news for the *New York Gazette*," Chester interrupted.

"Eh?" exclaimed Stubbs. "What's that? News? Sure, I've got to get some news. By George! Might be a good feature story up in those mountains." He turned to Colonel Edwards. "Count me in on this little trip, will you?" he said.

Colonel Edwards hesitated. He didn't know Stubbs as well as the others.

"Well—" he began.

"Oh, he's all right, Colonel," said Hal. "It's just his way. He's no coward. He is no more afraid than you are."

"Don't you believe it, Colonel," said Stubbs. "I assure you I am scared to death. But I am more afraid of losing my job with the *New York Gazette* than I am of these Albanian mountaineers, so if I go I am just choosing the lesser of two evils. I want to go with you fellows. But please remember one thing: I'm no fighter. If it comes to a fight, you can count me out; but if it's a question of run—well, you'll find me with you, or far ahead."

"Then if the others have no objections, I am sure that I shall be pleased to have you accompany us," said Colonel Edwards.

"And when shall we start?" asked Hal.

"Just as soon as we can."

"Walk, ride, or what?"

"Horses, until we reach the top of the mountains. Then we'll walk. Also, we will discard our uniforms—anyhow, I don't imagine you like the cut of those Austrian garments."

"I don't, and that's the truth," Hal agreed.

"Good. We'll change immediately. You go to my quarters and wait. I'll rustle up some civilian clothes and have them sent you. Also I'll arrange for our mounts and other details. I'll meet you here two hours from now."

With this Colonel Edwards betook himself away and the others returned to his quarters.

Half an hour later the clothes arrived and the four friends hastened to climb into them, Stubbs the while muttering to himself.

"Great Scott, Stubbs!" said Hal at last. "Quit your grumbling. Any one would think you were going to a funeral."

"And so I am—maybe," returned the little man. "And what worries me is that it is likely to be my own."

"You are a cheerful sort of a companion, I must say," declared Chester. "What's the use of yelling before you are hurt?"

"Because I probably won't be able to afterwards," was the reply.

Colonel Edwards was waiting when the four made their way to the appointed spot. The horses were picketed nearby.

"All ready?" asked the colonel. "Guns? Ammunition?"

All nodded.

"Then there is no use waiting longer. We may as well be moving."

He led the way to the horses and leaped lightly to the saddle. The others followed suit. Edwards waited until all were mounted and then headed his horse toward the north.

"Let us ride," he said.

All through the morning hours and well into the afternoon they rode along without adventure. They were challenged several times by Montenegrin outposts, but were allowed to proceed after an explanation by Colonel Edwards.

It was four o'clock by Hal's watch when Colonel Edwards at last drew rein in the far outskirts of a tiny mountain village.

"We'll leave our horses here," said the colonel, dismounting.

He led the way to a small barn near a smaller hut. Approaching the hut he gave a loud whistle. A man emerged and Colonel Edwards engaged him in conversation. At length the man nodded. Colonel Edwards turned to the others.

"We'll turn our horses over to him," he said. "I told him we would be back within seven days and wanted him to keep the animals here for us. He has agreed."

"But will he?" asked Hal.

Colonel Edwards shrugged his shoulders.

"You know as much about it as I do," he replied. "However, we have no choice."

"Well, they might come in handy if we get back," declared

Stubbs. "When we return this far we are liable to be in considerable of a hurry, and if the horses were not here it would be a terrible disappointment for us, at least. If we come back, we'll probably come on the run."

"And why will we come on the run?" Chester wanted to know.

"Bayonets behind,' returned Stubbs briefly. "Rifles, revolvers and whatnots. Oh, yes, we'll—"

"Stubbs," said Hal severely, "you would be a kill-joy at any feast. When it comes to plain, downright pessimism, you take the cake. Your equal does not exist."

"I'm glad to hear you say I'm good for something," muttered Stubbs.

"Well, if a pessimist is good for anything, you come first always," said Chester.

By this time the mountaineer had stabled their horses. Colonel Edwards gave him a piece of money, and mumbling his thanks, the man moved away.

"Which way?" asked Colonel Anderson.

Colonel Edwards drew a small map from his pocket, which he consulted for some moments.

"About five miles straight along this mountain road," he said at last. "There we cross the Albanian frontier, and there, also, we part company, or some of us do. Some of us will strike off to the right and the others to the left. You know what his majesty said. We would not learn much if we all went together."

"True," returned Hal. "Well, let's be moving."

They trudged along the rough, hilly road at a fair gait; but the walking was difficult and it was almost two hours later that Colonel Edwards again called a halt at what appeared to be a fork in the mountain pass.

"We'll split up here," he said briefly.

"And how?" asked Chester.

"That's up to you fellows. Of course, I'll take charge of one party, and I suppose Colonel Anderson should be entrusted with the other."

"Of course," said Chester. "I'll go with Colonel Anderson. Hal and Stubbs can go with you."

"One way as well as another," was the reply.

And so it was decided. There was a last handshake all around and the two parties went their separate ways—Colonel Anderson and Chester taking the more level trail to the right, and Colonel Edwards, Hal and Stubbs moving off along the rough pass to the left, leading more abruptly upward.

Clair W. Hayes

CHAPTER V

A SHOT FROM AMBUSH

Up, up and still up the road that Colonel Edwards, Hal and Stubbs had selected continued, winding first to the right and then to the left until all three had practically lost all sense of direction. Hal mentioned this.

"Don't know just where we are," he said.

"No," agreed Colonel Edwards. "However, it doesn't make much difference. We'll be around here for several days. Chances are the sun will come out before we get ready to leave and then we can get our bearings."

"Maybe there won't be any sun," said Stubbs.

"There you go again," said Hal. "Of course there'll be a sun. What's the use of hunting trouble?"

"I'm not hunting trouble," Stubbs disclaimed. "I just said maybe there won't be any sun."

Hal threw up both hands in a gesture of dismay.

"You're beyond hope," he declared.

After what seemed like hours of climbing, though in reality it was not more than two at the most, the three reached what apparently was the top of the mountain, and the road stretched out level ahead of them, heavily shaded on both sides with trees.

"Nice place for a fellow to hide and shoot a man," said Stubbs almost cheerfully.

Hal just looked at the little man but said nothing. Edwards grinned.

"Real cheerful little fellow, aren't you?" he said dryly.

Stubbs grinned back at him.

"I just said—" he began.

"We heard you," interrupted Hal.

The three trudged along silently for a few moments. Then, coming to a place where the trees crowded the road even closer and the branches hung low across their path, Stubbs again broke the silence.

"An assassin—" he began.

The interruption this time came from another source.

The little man's hat suddenly leaped from his head. There was the low whine of a bullet and a rifle cracked from the woods on the left.

Stubbs threw himself to the ground almost before his hat settled near him and he gave a loud cry.

"Help!"

Startled though they were by the unexpectedness of the attack, Colonel Edwards and Hal acted promptly. A revolver flashed in the hand of each and both fired into the woods toward the point from which the shot had come. Then they leaped for shelter among the trees that lined the road on the right. Stubbs, for the moment forgotten, still lay in the road and seemed to be attempting to bury his head in the dirt.

Hal, now sheltered by trees, perceived the little man's plight.

"Can't leave him there," he called to Edwards. "Cover me if you can."

Edwards nodded and held his revolver ready.

Hal dashed quickly from his shelter, grasped Stubbs by the right arm, jerked him violently to his feet and turned his face toward the woods on the right.

Stubbs seemed too frightened to realize in what direction lay safety, and breaking from Hal's hold, whirled about and dashed across the road, almost directly toward the spot from whence had come the shot a few moments before.

Hal gave a cry of dismay and dashed after him. But even as he would have given chase, there came a second rifle shot from the trees and Hal felt the breeze as a bullet sped by his ear. At the same moment Edwards yelled:

"Come back!"

Hal wasted no time in thought. He obeyed Edwards' command and dashed back to shelter with all speed.

"Whew!" he muttered. "That was pretty close."

"Rather," agreed Edwards dryly. "Where did the little man get to?"

"Oh, he's over there with our unseen enemy some place. He got away from me."

"I saw him," said Edwards grimly. "He's likely to have a warm time on the other side of the road."

Hal grinned in spite of himself, as he replied:

"He is that. I suppose we should do something to help him, but I am frank to say I don't know just what."

"We'll have to figure some way to get rid of that fellow," said Edwards. "He's dangerous. Apparently there is only one."

"Tell you what," said Hal, "you stick here. I'll sneak through the trees here for a quarter of a mile, cross the road and double back. If I can go quietly enough perhaps I can catch him off his guard."

Edwards considered this plan.

"Might be done," he said finally. "I don't think of anything else. Off with you then."

Hal walked still deeper into the woods and then turned to his left. Keeping himself well screened from the road he made his way carefully and silently along. At last, when he felt sure that he could no longer be seen by their unexpected foe, he approached the road again.

The lad poked his head out cautiously and, after a quick glance back to make sure there was no one in sight, crossed the road at a bound, almost expecting as he did so to hear a bullet whiz near.

No bullet came.

Once safe on the other side, the lad turned again to his left and doubled back. He went more cautiously now, making sure of each footstep that he might not warn the unseen foe of his approach.

In the woods there was the silence of death.

Hal, moving slowly forward, now felt that he must have reached the point from which the two shots had been fired and stopped and listened intently. Once he thought he heard the sound of a snapping twig and became perfectly quiet, waiting for the sound to be repeated; but it did not come again.

"Guess I must have been mistaken," the lad told himself, as he moved forward again.

Five minutes later Hal stopped suddenly in his tracks. He had heard a sound close at hand and knew he was not mistaken this time. A twig had snapped perhaps twenty yards to his right and as far ahead.

Hal grasped his automatic more firmly.

"Hope I get the first shot," he muttered.

Suddenly he caught sight of a form as it flitted from one tree to another. Quickly the lad raised his revolver and fired.

There was no outcry, and looking again, the lad saw no one.

"Missed him," he muttered. "Well, I've betrayed myself! Now I'll have to be more careful."

He lay down upon the ground behind the tree where he had taken shelter and waited patiently. Ten minutes later he thought he saw an object move behind a tree a scant fifteen yards away.

Again the lad fired.

This shot was followed by a startled cry as a figure leaped to its feet and started off through the woods at full speed.

Hal sprang to his feet.

"Halt!" he cried.

The figure seemed to run faster than before.

Hal paused and leveled his revolver in deliberate aim. His finger tightened on the trigger—then, suddenly he let his arm fall.

"Stubbs!" he cried in amazement.

The running figure was indeed the little war correspondent.

"By Jove!" muttered Hal. "Another moment and I would have shot him." He raised his voice in a shout: "Hey, Stubbs!"

But the little man ran on, unheeding.

"He'll run right smack into that other fellow if he doesn't watch out," Hal told himself. "Well, I suppose I'll have to

Clair W. Hayes

stop him."

Still holding his revolver in his right hand, he also broke into a run and made after the fleeing Stubbs.

Several times he called, but Stubbs paid no heed. Then Hal grew angry.

"I'll get you if I have to chase you right back to the door of the *New York Gazette*" he muttered to himself.

He gained at every stride and was rapidly overtaking the war correspondent, although Stubbs, with head lowered, looking neither to the right nor to the left, his arms working like pistons, ran blindly on.

Suddenly Hal stopped almost in his tracks and his heart leaped into his throat.

From behind a tree directly in Stubbs' path, stepped a short squat figure, with great long arms dangling at its side. A revolver was clasped in the right hand and the weapon was slowly raised until it covered Stubbs.

Hal gave a loud cry of warning, raised his own revolver and fired. But even as his finger tightened on the trigger he knew he had missed. Stubbs was so close to the other figure that the lad had been afraid of hitting him. Consequently the bullet went wild.

But though it missed its mark, Hal's bullet undoubtedly saved Stubbs' life, for it attracted the attention of the enemy for a brief moment; and in that moment, Anthony Stubbs, still unaware of the danger that confronted him, dashed head first into his would-be slayer.

So great was the force of the impact that both were hurled to the ground. With rare presence of mind, Stubbs, recovering his breath before his unexpected opponent realized what had happened, reached out and procured the other's revolver and hurled it aside.

Then he attempted to get to his feet, but at this point the other came back to life and seized him by the legs.

"Hey! Leggo my legs!" shouted Stubbs.

The other held him tightly.

"Let me up!" cried Stubbs again.

Still the other clung fast, while Stubbs raised a cry for help.

At this juncture Hal reached the combatants. He was about to lend a hand, when he saw that Stubbs' opponent was unarmed, and drew back.

Stubbs did not see him, and apparently believing that he was to get no help, he turned to give battle. He kicked out with his left foot and the foot came free. He followed suit with the right foot and felt it strike something soft. At the same moment there came a cry of pain from Stubbs' opponent and the grasp upon his other leg relaxed.

Quickly the little man leaped to his feet and darted toward the spot where he had thrown the revolver. He snatched it up and leveled it at his adversary.

"Hands up there!" he called.

There came a choking cry from the queer figure and the long arms were raised high in the air.

Clair W. Hayes

"Good for you, Stubbs!" cried Hal at this juncture.

Stubbs gazed about sharply.

"About time you were getting here," he said. "I had a terrible fight with this fellow."

CHAPTER VI

A STRANGE ENCOUNTER

Hal laughed aloud.

"Terrible fight, eh?" he exclaimed. "Of course you did. What else could you do? You had to fight. Pretty lucky, Stubbs."

"Lucky!" echoed Stubbs. "What do you mean, lucky? If you had been here in time to see me tackle this fellow you would have known what a hard time I had."

"I saw you," replied Hal. "You can put down your gun, now. I'll take care of this fellow."

He leveled his own revolver at the queer-looking creature before him and Stubbs placed his newly-acquired revolver in his coat pocket.

Hal motioned to his prisoner to approach. The latter did so with an ugly scowl on his face. He seemed not to have the slightest fear and came up to the lad unflinchingly.

"Speak English?" asked Hal.

There was no reply.

Clair W. Hayes

"French?"

The man nodded.

"Who are you?" demanded Hal.

"Nikol."

"Nikol what?"

The man did not reply, and Hal surveyed him critically. He was at least thirty-five years of age, could not have been an inch more than four feet in height, and his long, knotted arms, apparently as strong as a gorilla's, reached almost to the ground, where his huge hand clasped and unclasped nervously. Involuntarily Hal shuddered.

"Must be as strong as an ox," the lad muttered. "Lucky for Stubbs he kicked at the right time and happened to land."

"What's your last name?" the lad demanded again.

"Haven't any," was the reply.

"What are you, an Albanian?"

"Yes."

"What are you doing here?"

The man did not reply.

Stubbs had been an interesting listener to the conversation and became decidedly impatient when the dwarf refused to answer Hal's questions.

"Why don't you speak?" he demanded aggressively, taking a step forward. He felt perfectly safe now that Hal had the man covered.

Instantly there was an unexpected change in the dwarf's manner. He stepped back a pace and bowed his head before the angry Stubbs.

"I did not know that you wished me to answer," he replied civilly. "I will talk to you, for you are the first man who has ever conquered me; and you are a small man, too—a dwarf."

"What's that?" exclaimed Stubbs still more angrily, for "the dwarf" had touched upon a tender spot. "Dwarf, am I? What do you mean by talking to me like that?"

Again he took a step forward and the Albanian drew back.

"You will please excuse me," he said humbly. "I did not mean to offend. For myself I am proud that I am a dwarf and I was glad that it was one of my own kind who conquered me."

Stubbs, greatly flattered, threw out his chest and turned to Hal.

"You see," he exclaimed, "if you have any doubts as to how I overcame this man, he will tell you himself. Won't you, Nik—Nikol?"

Nikol bowed.

"I will, sir," he replied.

"Well, you seem to have done a good job," Hal replied. "I don't believe I could have overcome him. In fact, I am sure of it. Now if you will kindly order your newly made slave to answer my questions, perhaps we may learn something."

Stubbs gave the order in the tone of a man born to command and the dwarf nodded his understanding.

"If my boss knew I could give orders like that, I'd have a better job," was Stubbs' comment as Hal turned to Nikol.

"What are your sympathies in this war?" asked the lad quietly.

"My sympathies," was the reply, "I have kept locked up here," and Nikol tapped his breast with one of his huge fingers. "But, now that my conqueror requests me to talk, I will tell you. My sympathies are with Montenegro; always have been and always will be."

"Good!" exclaimed Hal. "Then perhaps you can tell me something of the Austrian sentiment in these mountains."

"The Austrian sympathy is very strong," was the reply. "Not so much here as further north. Thousands of tribesmen there are only awaiting the arrival of the Austrians to join their ranks. Some have joined already."

"And is there not danger for a man of your sympathies in these parts?"

The Albanian shrugged his shoulders.

"I have said," he replied, "that I keep my sympathies locked up here," and again he tapped his breast.

Hal was silent for a few moments, considering a plan that had come to him. At length he turned to Stubbs.

"Will you ask your newly made friend," he said, "if he will join us? He will be invaluable. He can lead us where we would go without question."

Stubbs grasped the situation instantly.

He put the question to the Albanian. For long minutes the man hesitated, and then he, in turn, asked a question.

"You say that you are working in the interests of Montenegro?" he asked.

"I can give you my word," replied Stubbs soberly.

The dwarf extended a hand to Stubbs and looked him in the eye.

"Such men as you, such fighters as you, do not lie," he said gravely.

Stubbs blushed like a schoolboy as he extended a hand, which was seized in a grip that brought tears to the little man's eyes. But he bore the pain bravely, for he did not wish to lose caste in the eyes of his new admirer.

"Come then," said Hal. "We'll pick up Colonel Edwards again and be moving."

He led the way back to where the first shot had been fired and raised his voice in a shout:

"All right, Edwards?"

"All right," was the reply.

"I've caught the enemy," explained Hal. "You can come from

under cover."

He led the way to the road and a moment later Colonel Edwards joined them.

"What have we here?" he exclaimed, after a glance at the dwarf.

"A guide," replied Hal; "the same being the man who fired at us, and also Stubbs' own prisoner."

"Stubbs' prisoner?"

"Exactly. He captured him single-handed."

Colonel Edwards eyed Stubbs in the greatest surprise, until Hal explained in a low voice, so that neither Stubbs nor the dwarf might hear.

"Well, we may as well be moving then," said Colonel Edwards. "Have your guide take the lead, Stubbs."

Stubbs, undeniably proud at the honor now being bestowed upon him, did as requested, and the dwarf led the way down the road at a rapid gait.

Hour after hour they walked along encountering no one, until shortly before nightfall when they drew up near a small hut. Here Nikol went forward and secured food, which he brought back in his hands. This they devoured hungrily, drank from a little brook, and moved forward again.

Now Nikol deserted the beaten path and struck off through the mountains proper, climbing steep hills, leaping ruts and gullies, rocks and brooks, but making such good progress that the others were hard pressed to keep up with him.

Darkness fell suddenly and Stubbs shuddered.

"Nice place for an assassin here, too," he muttered gloomily.

"Back at it, are you?" said Hal. "What will your friend Nikol say?"

Stubbs did not reply.

Suddenly the dwarf halted and motioned the others to silence. All listened intently and directly made out what the sharp ears of Nikol had caught first—the sound of approaching footsteps.

Nikol motioned the others back into the shadow of a great rock and stepped boldly forward. Then he hesitated a moment, came back and spoke to Stubbs in a low voice, yet loud enough for the others to hear.

"If I should chance to be outmatched," he said, "you will come to my assistance? The others," he snapped his fingers, "are no good. You will come?"

Taken wholly off his guard, Stubbs stuttered and stammered.

"You will come?" Nikol repeated again.

"Ye-e-s, I'll come," Stubbs articulated at last.

Nikol wasted no further time in words, but moved forward perhaps a hundred yards. Then he halted and stood still, waiting.

The sound of footsteps drew nearer and still nearer, and then suddenly Nikol sprang forward, silently and swiftly.

There came a sudden startled cry from ahead and then a great, boisterous laugh.

"Ho! Ho!" exclaimed a voice in French. "Look what has attacked Ivan Vergoff."

For some reason that he could not explain, Hal left his place of concealment and moved toward the combatants. The others followed him.

"Ho! Ho!" came the great voice again. "Ivan Vergoff, the greatest of the Cossacks, attacked by this puny pygmy."

Hal had now approached close enough to see the gigantic figure of Nikol's antagonist and to witness the struggle.

The giant had stooped over and seized Nikol by one arm. He pulled, but the dwarf, his feet firmly planted on the ground, did not budge. It was a great exhibition of strength, for Hal knew that the stranger must be a powerful man.

This time the giant did not laugh.

"A strong man," he muttered aloud. "A strong man, though he be a pygmy."

He now extended another arm, seized the dwarf around the middle and lifted him high above his head. With his right arm the dwarf struck the face that gazed up at him as he was suspended high in the air.

The big man gave a roar like that of an angry bull, hurled the dwarf from him and then jumped after the flying figure with remarkable agility for a man of his huge size.

But even as he would have seized Nikol again, Hal

stepped forward.

"Wait!" cried the lad, who had been doing some quick thinking. "Your name is Ivan Vergoff and you are a Cossack?"

The big man paused suddenly and glanced about him.

"Yes!" he shouted. "What of it?"

"Only," replied Hal quietly, "that I bring you word of your brother, Alexis!"

Clair W. Hayes

CHAPTER VII

NEW FRIENDS

The big man paused and turned an enquiring eye upon Hal, whom he could dimly perceive in the darkness.

"Alexis!" he echoed. "What of him? How do you know I have a brother Alexis?"

Hal replied rapidly in the Russian dialect which he had picked up during his service with the Cossacks, as told in the story of "The Boy Allies With the Cossacks," while the man listened intently. Then the giant set the dwarf upon his feet remarking:

"Now, you just stay there a little while. I may have more to say to you later, but right now I would know something of my brother Alexis, whom I have not seen in years. And my brother Stephan, also, what do you know of him?" he demanded of Hal.

The lad shook his head.

"Not much," he said. "But come, we'll find some spot where we can make a fire and I'll tell you what I know of Alexis."

"Good," boomed the big man. "Follow me."

Without another word he turned on his heel and strode away whence he had come. The other four followed him, Nikol the while muttering angrily to himself.

Stubbs turned upon him suddenly.

"What's the matter with you?" he demanded. "Don't you know it's cold here? I want to sit by the fire awhile. Keep still."

The dwarf made no reply, but became silent. It was plain enough that he stood very much in awe of Stubbs.

After a five-minute walk through the dark woods, the big Cossack wheeled sharply to the left, and walking swiftly for perhaps fifty yards drew up before what appeared to be a solid rock.

Looking closer in the darkness, however, Hal saw a slight opening at the bottom, the space between the rock and the ground being perhaps three feet. The rock, apparently, rested upon more solid ground farther back.

"Follow me," said the big man again.

He dropped on his hands and knees and wriggled through the opening.

At this point Stubbs manifested a desire to leave the others in the lurch.

"Say!" he exclaimed. "You're not going to get me under there. How do you know what he may have in mind to do to us?"

Clair W. Hayes

"Come, Stubbs," said Hal. "Don't be a quitter all the time. Nothing is going to hurt—"

Before he could finish his sentence he felt himself seized in a powerful grip from behind. He twisted about with an effort and looked down upon the scowling face of Nikol.

"Here! What's the matter?" he cried.

The dwarf grinned at him evilly, and still retaining his hold, gazed at Stubbs.

"He insulted you," he said. "What shall I do with him?"

"Great Scott! Let him down!" exclaimed the little man, anxiously. "He didn't do anything to me."

"But he insulted you," protested Nikol. "I heard him say—"

"Oh, that was just in fun," cried Stubbs. "Let him go."

The dwarf's hold relaxed and Hal jumped away.

"Don't try any of that on me again," he said, facing Nikol angrily. He turned to Stubbs. "You just instruct this fellow to keep his hands off me, or I shall have to take my gun to him."

"Oh, he didn't mean any harm," Stubbs protested.

"Maybe he didn't and maybe he did," replied Hal. "At any rate, I don't like that kind of treatment. You tell him what I said."

"He was just sticking up for me," said Stubbs, aggrievedly. "But I'll tell him."

He did so, but the dwarf said nothing.

At this juncture the big Cossack poked his head from beneath the rock.

"Are you coming in here or not?" he demanded in a gruff voice.

"Coming," said Hal, dropping to his knees.

"Look here, Hal," said Stubbs, "I don't like the looks of this place. Maybe we had better stay outside."

"Nonsense," Edwards spoke up at this point. "The man means us no harm."

Hal had disappeared beneath the rock and Edwards dropped to his knees and crawled after him.

"Well," said Stubbs to himself, "I don't like this, but I guess I might as well go along."

Motioning Nikol to follow him, he, too, dropped to all fours and crawled slowly beneath the big rock.

Beyond the rock, a brisk fire made dimly visible what appeared to be a large cavern. The fire seemed to be in the exact center of a large underground room and beyond it Hal thought he could make out the mouths of dark passageways that led off in several directions.

"Come up to the fire and get warm," the big Cossack invited.

The others accepted the invitation, first discarding their heavy outer garments. When all appeared comfortable, the big Cossack spoke.

"Now," he said, addressing Hal, "tell me of Alexis. He is—"

"Dead," Hal interrupted quietly.

Ivan sprang to his feet.

"Dead!" he shouted. "And you dare to tell it to me? You, no doubt, had a hand in his death!"

"On the contrary," returned the lad quietly, "I tried to save him, as did my chum; but it was too late. But he died like a brave man and a true Cossack."

Ivan was silent for several moments, and then said sneeringly:

"And what do you know of the Cossacks?"

"Well, very little, to be sure," Hal confessed, "though, for a short time, I had the honor of serving in a Cossack regiment."

"What, you?" exclaimed Ivan incredulously. "Impossible."

"No; what I say is true," said Hal. "And it was there that I met your brother Alexis, than whom I have never seen a braver man."

"'Tis true," muttered Ivan. "Alexis was ever a brave man, though much given to boasting. Also, barring perhaps myself, he was the most powerful man I have ever seen."

"He was indeed," replied Hal, "and it will give me pleasure at some time to relate to you some of the remarkable feats I have seen him accomplish."

"Alexis has related enough," returned Ivan dryly. "But come, now, tell me what you know of him."

"Well," Hal began, "I met Alexis first—"

He stopped suddenly and listened attentively.

"What was that?" he demanded.

"What?" asked Edwards.

"I thought I heard a voice calling. Sounded like a cry for help."

Ivan broke into a loud laugh.

"Ho! Ho!" he cried. "Guess you heard my prisoners."

"Prisoners?" Hal repeated inquiringly.

"Yes. I came across them this afternoon. They sought to ply me with questions. I treated them respectfully enough, but when they continued to plague me, I just picked them up and brought them here. I have a suspicion they may be Austrian spies and if there is one race of men for whom I have no use, it is the Austrians. But they do not annoy you, do they? If so, I shall go back and have a word with them. After that I assure you they will annoy you no more."

"Oh, no," Hal hastened to say. "They do not annoy me in the slightest. But what do you intend to do with them?"

"Well, I don't know exactly," returned Ivan. "You know I have read somewhat, and I remember the things I have read. For instance now, I would like to be like one of the old kings, or say even a present-day American, of whom I have heard much. They have slaves and things. Why not make my prisoners my slaves?"

"I assure you you are wrong about the Americans," said Hal. "I chance to be one myself, so I know. Of kings, I cannot say."

"Never mind," said Ivan. "We'll attend to them later on. Right now I have a desire to hear your story. Proceed."

Hal did so. He related his and Chester's first meeting with Alexis, the big brave-hearted man who had once played an important part in their lives, as related in "The Boy Allies With the Cossacks." He told of the many exciting adventures the three had gone through together.

And as the lad progressed with his narrative, Ivan became more interested with each word; and by the time Hal had come to an account of his brother's last great fight, Ivan was on his feet, his face glowing.

"By St. George!" he cried. "I knew he could do it. Boaster or not, he was a brave man. But go on. And after he had killed the three Germans there on the sand, then what?"

"Why, then," said Hal, "a German bullet struck him in the right shoulder; a moment later another lodged in his right side. But Alexis did not pause. He rushed right into the thick of them, using his now empty pistols and at last striking out with his bare fists. Men tumbled on all sides.

"From behind and from both sides, the Germans darted at him, firing their revolvers and stabbing him with the swords. By this time, we had finished repairing our machine and we rushed to his aid, and for a moment the Germans gave back. Then they closed in and we were all hard pressed. Alexis was bleeding in a dozen places but he fought on. And then aid came from an unexpected source."

"Where?" demanded Ivan excitedly.

"Troops," replied Hal. "Troops sent to protect the neutrality of the country; and with their approach the Germans who were still upon their feet fled. Chester and I dragged Alexis to our own craft and we also ascended. There we did what we could for him, but he realized that he was past aid, and he died as a brave man should. We buried him in England with honor, and with him the Cross of St. George, personally bestowed upon him by the Czar."

For a long time after the lad had finished, Ivan was silent. Then he said, his fists clenching:

"I would I had been there! There would have been a different story to tell!"

Hal was about to reply, but a voice sounded suddenly. Hal pricked up his ears. Surely he recognized that voice. The cry came again.

"Chester!" shouted Hal, and sprang to his feet.

CHAPTER VIII

A DESPERATE VENTURE

Before Ivan could raise a hand to stay him, had such been his intention, Hal had darted across the cavern in the direction from which had come the sound he had recognized as Chester's voice. It was very dark there and the lad could not make out his surroundings, but he seemed to have brought up against a solid wall. He explored the smooth surface with his hands, but could find no opening in that particular spot. Then he came upon one of the narrow passageways and entered it without hesitation, for he believed it was in that direction he would find Chester.

Now heavy footsteps sounded behind him and Ivan's voice roared:

"Where are you going?"

"It is Chester—my friend who was with me when Alexis died," returned Hal. "I heard his voice. He must be near some place and in trouble."

"Ho!" said Ivan. "He will be one of my prisoners, I expect. I remember that one was rather young."

"Well, let him out, will you?" exclaimed Hal.

"Certainly," returned Ivan.

He passed Hal and led the way down the dark passage. Presently Hal heard a huge rock move and then footsteps came toward him.

"Who is it?" he asked.

There came a cry of surprise.

"That you, Hal?" came in Chester's voice. "How on earth did you get here?"

"That's rather a long story," replied Hal, "but it seems that it's a good thing I did get here. I thought a heard a sound awhile back. It must have been you."

"Anderson and I have been yelling for the last week, it seems," said Chester ruefully. "We didn't hope to be fortunate enough to raise you, but we thought some one might hear us."

"Well, come on out here to the fire—and you, too, Colonel," his last to Colonel Anderson, who now came forward, closely followed by Ivan.

They needed no urging, for they had been shut up in the cold so long that they were almost frozen. Introductions now followed all around and Ivan seemed genuinely pleased to meet Chester. He was profuse in his apologies for his rough treatment, while Chester was dumbfounded to learn that his captor was the brother of his old friend Alexis. They shook hands heartily.

Clair W. Hayes

"If you had not pestered me with so many questions, I would not have bothered you," Ivan explained. "To tell the truth, I took you for a couple of Austrian spies."

"Tell us, Chester," said Hal, "what have you learned?"

"Learned?" echoed Chester. "We haven't learned anything, except that it is awfully cold in these mountains. I'm going to tell you right now, it's no fun being locked up in an icebox."

"It is not," Colonel Anderson agreed dryly, stretching his feet out to the fire.

"I'll tell you how it came about," said Chester, smiling at Ivan. "Colonel Anderson and I had just completed a most terrible climb. Coming once again to a level spot we sat down to rest. We saw a man coming along—a big man, none other than Ivan here. I suggested that we ask him a few questions."

"You asked them, all right," said Ivan.

"Well," Chester continued, "he didn't tell us much. In fact, he was as mum as an oyster. Colonel Anderson took a hand with no better luck. It seems that between us we talked too much. Ivan here didn't like it. He said he guessed he'd have to take us along with him. We said we were satisfied to stay where we were. This didn't suit Ivan. He reached for me and I dodged; but with his other hand he grabbed Anderson and held him helpless.

"I drew my gun but I was afraid to fire for fear of hitting the Colonel. I thought I would rap the big man over the head with the butt of the weapon. I ventured a trifle too close and he nailed me, too. He shook me so hard that I dropped my gun. Anderson hadn't been able to get at his. Then Ivan relieved him of it, and still holding us each by an arm, he brought us here.

"When he shoved us under the rock ahead of him, we decided to jump him if he came in. We jumped him. It didn't do much good, did it, Colonel?"

Chester turned to Colonel Anderson with a smile.

"Not much," was the Colonel's dry response.

Ivan grinned sheepishly.

"I didn't mean to hurt you too much," he said. "You see, sometimes I don't realize my own strength. I guess maybe I squeezed your arms too hard."

"Well, now tell us about yourself, Hal," said Chester, "and who is this little fellow who hangs so close to Stubbs?"

"This little fellow," returned Hal, "has appointed himself Stubbs' best friend. Stubbs overcame him in fair fight this afternoon and he thinks Stubbs is a great man."

"Well, what's the matter?" Stubbs broke in. "Don't you?"

"Of course," Hal hastened to assure him.

Stubbs subsided grumbling.

"The question now is," Colonel Edwards declared, "what are we going to do? There is no use staying here longer than we can possibly help. We had better be moving."

"Hold on," shouted Ivan, jumping suddenly to his feet. "Tell me what it is you are going to do? Perhaps I may lend a hand. I know something of these mountains."

Colonel Edwards glanced at Hal. The boy nodded.

"Might be a good idea," he said.

Then Colonel Edwards explained. Ivan heard him patiently.

"Well," he said at length, "nothing would please me more than to join this expedition." He spoke to Hal. "You have told me of the service rendered the Czar by my brother Alexis. I am ashamed that I have been idling here in these mountains while my country needs me. I shall try and make up for it in the future. Now, I believe I can tell you what you want to know."

"Then," asked Colonel Edwards, "is there a strong Austrian sentiment among the Albanians?"

"Until a month ago there was little Austrian sentiment," returned Ivan, "But recently there has been a change, and the change I lay at the door of a single man."

"An Albanian?"

"It is even worse than that. The man is a Montenegrin. And still worse. He bears the same name as the king of Montenegro, Nicolas. He has, most likely, another name, but I do not know it."

"But why should a Montenegrin seek to raise the enmity of the Albanians against his own people?" Chester demanded.

"There is but one reason—gold," said Ivan simply.

"And his methods?" inquired Colonel Anderson.

"More gold," was the reply.

"I see," said Colonel Anderson. "Furnished by the Austrians, eh?"

"How else? I have had several interviews with this Nicolas. He seems to think I could be of use to him. In fact, he has made me offers. But while I have taken no part in active fighting, although I admit I have neglected my own country, I have not fallen low enough for that sort of work. However, I did not tell Nicolas that. I temporized with him and I suppose he believes he can win me over if he cares to make his offer tempting enough."

"All this," said Hal slowly, "suggests a plan."

"Well?" said Chester, expectantly.

"And by this plan of mine," Hal continued, "we may accomplish even more than we set out to do."

"Explain, Hal," said Colonel Anderson.

"It's very simple. We'll have Ivan take us to Nicolas. He can tell him we are Germans, or what you please. Being, apparently, friends of Ivan's, we shall be received. Then Ivan can appear to fall in with his plans. At the first opportune moment, we shall take charge of Mr. Nicolas and escape."

"H-m-m-m," mused Colonel Edwards. "You say all that easily enough, but you can take my word for it, it will be no small job."

"Of course not," Chester agreed, "but still we should be able to do it. And if we do, we shall have removed the cause of the Albanian enmity toward Montenegro. There will be no

Clair W. Hayes

such strong Austrian sentiment once the supply of gold is cut off."

Ivan jumped to his feet and clapped the lad on the back.

"Good!" he exclaimed eagerly. "I'm with you; and if it comes to a fight, you will find that you can use me to advantage."

"I am sure of it," smiled Hal.

Ivan, in turning, cast his eye upon the little dwarfed figure of Nikol. He walked quickly toward him and extended a hand.

"We didn't finish our little argument awhile ago," he said simply. "I see no reason why we should finish it. Why should we fight each other when there are others to fight?" He turned to Hal. "I'll guarantee this man will give a good account of himself," he said. "I doubt if there is another man in the mountains, besides myself, who has his strength. He will prove his worth."

He turned to Nikol again and the dwarf grinned at him, showing strong white teeth.

"You are right," he said and gripped Ivan's hand hard.

"Well then," said Colonel Edwards, "the sooner we get started the sooner we may get back again. When shall we start, Ivan?"

"Immediately," was the reply, and the giant moved toward the mouth of the cavern.

"Now, look-a-here, you fellows," said the voice of Anthony Stubbs. "I've been a whole lot of places with you and I hope to go with you a whole lot more, but I claim it is downright foolishness to stick our heads into a brigand's lair. What's the use? The best we can get is the worst of it."

"Stubbs," said Hal quietly, "you don't have to go along if you don't want to. You can stay right here."

"What?" exclaimed the little man. "Stay here by myself? I should say not. I don't want to stay here alone and I don't want to go hunting brigands. What I want to do is get some place where it's safe. I don't like this country, if you want to know it."

"It's a good country," said Nikol abruptly.

Stubbs looked at the dwarf in surprise. It was the first time the Albanian had talked back to him.

"What do you know about it?" demanded Stubbs. "You never saw a regular country."

The dwarf bowed his head in some confusion. Apparently Stubbs' spell still held good over him.

"Come, Stubbs, don't be stubborn," said Chester.

"Well, all right," said the little man, shaking his head sadly. "I'll go if the rest of you do, but I want to tell you right now, I protest!"

CHAPTER IX

THE TRAITOR

"If I am not mistaken," said Ivan, "here comes Nicolas now."

He pointed to a large, bearded individual, who, surrounded by probably a dozen other figures, was advancing toward them. The man swung along with the free and easy stride of the mountaineer, looking neither to the right nor to the left, his head erect and of haughty mien.

"Pompous sort of a looking customer," said Colonel Anderson to Hal.

"Rather," said the lad dryly. He glanced at the others, Colonel Edwards, Stubbs, Nikol, Ivan and Chester, and muttered hurriedly: "After this we must do all our talking in German."

The others nodded their understanding and all fell silent as the Montenegrin traitor and his henchmen approached.

It was the morning following the night upon which they had left Ivan's retreat. The journey had consumed the whole night, but in spite of their fatigue, each member of the party of seven was on his mettle. Now, as Nicolas drew closer,

Ivan took a step in advance of the others to greet him.

The traitor's face lighted with pleasure as he recognized the big Cossack.

"Ah, Ivan," he said, "I am glad to see you."

He noticed the others, and a slight frown flitted across his face. He swept his arm toward them in a comprehensive gesture. "Who are these?"

"One of them you probably know," said Ivan and he indicated Nikol.

Nikol nodded affirmatively.

"The others," Ivan continued, "I came across in the mountains last night. They are Germans and were seeking you."

"Seeking me?" exclaimed Nicolas in astonishment. "And why should they be seeking me?"

"You will probably know," returned Ivan, "when I tell you they come from Germany."

"Ah," said Nicolas. "Of course I know, Ivan. Will you have them come forward?"

"One moment, Nicolas," said Ivan. "First I would have a word with you myself."

"Proceed," said the Montenegrin.

"Well, then," Ivan went on, "you may remember a certain proposal you have made me upon several occasions?"

"I do," exclaimed Nicolas, with unfeigned eagerness. "Can it be that at last you have decided to—"

"Accept?" interrupted Ivan. "Yes; I have decided to accept; and these Germans here have had something to do with my decision. They have told me how Germany and Austria combined will eventually win the great war and of the good things that will be in store for all of us when that day comes. You are right, Nicolas, it is well to be on the winning side."

"And I am glad you see it that way," declared Nicolas, extending a hand, which Ivan grasped, much to his distaste. "I have long wanted a trusted lieutenant, and you shall be he."

"Thanks, Nicolas," returned Ivan. "I had not expected that. Had you told me before it might have influenced me sooner. But now I shall have the others approach. By the way, you speak German?"

"Yes."

"Good; then there is no need of an interpreter."

He raised his hand and at the signal the others came forward. Ivan presented each in turn, applying to each a German name that had been agreed upon during the night's travel. Nicolas expressed his pleasure at seeing them and after a few words of pleasantry, said:

"Now, gentlemen, if you will accompany me to my quarters. I shall try and make you feel at home."

As they walked along Hal and Chester took stock of the Montenegrin. Big he was, fully as tall and as broad as Ivan himself, and his great arms hung below his knees. He was the personification of rugged strength and brutality. From Nicolas the lads turned their eyes to Ivan. There was scarcely a noticeable difference in the stature of the two men and from casual observation it would have been hard to choose between them in the matter of strength. But the one noticeable difference was in the eyes.

Ivan's eyes looked one straight in the face, while Nicolas' shifted uneasily when he was observed closely. It was the difference in the eyes that told the difference between the two men better than anything else.

Presently Nicolas stopped before an extremely large hut, built up close beside a giant rock. He stood aside and motioned the others to enter. They did so and Nicolas, after a word to his men, came in after them and closed the door. Then he motioned them all to seats and sat down himself. He eyed his guests in silence for a few moments, and finally remarked:

"Well?"

Hal took it upon himself to do the talking.

"First," he said, "we would like to know how you are progressing?"

"Beautifully," was Nicolas' reply. "I have distributed the gold given me for that purpose, first, of course, taking out my own share. The Albanians, knowing the poverty of the Montenegrins, have been convinced by the gold that final success in this war must crown the Austrian arms. Austrian sentiment is becoming greater each day. But I need more money."

"That is what we have come to see you about," said Hal.

"You see, that while you are well informed as to just what is going on here, we have only your word for it. You may be telling the truth—and you may be lying."

Nicolas jumped to his feet, his fingers twitching.

"You dare—" he began.

"Nonsense," said Hal, remaining perfectly quiet. "This is no time for heroics. I have come here to find out something and I am going to find it out. Now how much of this gold have you given out as ordered, and how much have you kept for yourself?"

"I—I—well, I have—" Nicholas began.

"As I thought," said Hal. "You have been holding out. We can't have anything like that, you know. Where is the gold?"

Nicolas, for a moment, seemed about to make a denial, but Hal eyed him steadily, and he said at last:

"It is under this floor here," and he tapped the floor with his foot.

"All right," said Hal. "In shape to be carried?"

"Why yes, I guess half a dozen men could carry it well enough."

"I am glad to hear that," said Hal, "because I want you to dig it out right now."

Again Nicolas started to protest, but apparently thinking better of it, changed his mind and said:

"It shall be as you say. But you will not hold this against me, my having held some of the gold for my own?"

"Not if you do as I say."

"And I shall have more gold?"

"We shall see; perhaps."

"Then I shall uncover the other," said Nicolas.

He stooped to his knees and lifted a loose board in the floor.

"One moment," said Hal. "Your men outside. We can take no chances with them. If they knew you had all this gold stored here there would be a fight. Step outside and tell them to go away."

This time Nicolas obeyed without even hesitating.

While he was outside, Hal whispered quickly to the others:

"There is no use delaying. We'll give his men time to get out of hearing and then we'll grab him."

"But the gold, what are you going to do with that?" Ivan wanted to know.

Hal smiled a bit.

"I don't know how I happened to think of that," he said, "but now that we practically have it in our hands, I vote that we turn it over to the impoverished little kingdom of Montenegro."

"By Jove! Good!" exclaimed Colonel Edwards. "My boy,

you have a wonderful head on your shoulders. I am proud to know you."

"Thanks," said Hal. "Now, as long as I have been doing the talking, I may as well continue. We'll keep quiet until we are sure this traitor's men are out of earshot and then we'll take possession of Mr. Nicolas and his unearned gold."

A few moments later Nicolas re-entered the hut.

"Get rid of them?" asked Hal, briefly.

"Yes."

"Good. Then get busy and bring your gold out."

"Look here," said Nicolas, eyeing Hal somewhat angrily. "I don't like your tone exactly."

"I don't exactly care whether you do or not," returned Hal quietly. "You are pretty small fry in this game, Nicolas, and I'm not afraid of you. Remember, if anything should happen to me, you'll have the German government on your trail, and then what would you do for gold?"

Nicolas opened his mouth to reply; then thought better of it and closed his lips without uttering a sound.

"All right, now that we understand each other," said Hal. "Get to work and produce the gold."

Nicolas waited no further, but did as commanded.

"One," counted Hal, as the man drew from beneath the board a little sack of gold.

One after another Hal counted them as they were laid on the floor at his feet, until in all there were seventeen little sacks, just small enough to permit of being stowed away in outside coat pockets.

"Two for each of us to carry," said Hal, looking around, "and one over. I'll carry the extra one in my hand."

"And don't I get any of this?" demanded Nicolas, looking at the bags of gold longingly.

"You do not," replied Hal, quietly. "This money is to be given where it will do the most good. You have had your chance with it. Now it is my turn."

"Very well," said Nicolas, with a shrug of his shoulders. "But I have made my agreement with the Austrian government; and when the war has been won, I shall get my pay."

"Perhaps," said Hal, with a double meaning, that was, of course, lost upon Nicolas, "you shall receive your just pay before the war ends."

"Do you really think so?" asked Nicolas eagerly. "I hope so."

"But now," said Hal, "it is time to be moving. Pick up the gold, men, and let's get away from here."

The others obeyed. Each stowed two sacks in his pocket and Hal carried the seventeenth package in his hand. Then Hal motioned them out the door. He emerged after them and his hand was on his automatic as he did so.

"Which way?" asked Chester.

"Straight ahead," said Nicolas.

"No," said Hal quietly. "About face. We are going the other way."

"Where to?" demanded Nicolas surlily.

"Right back to Cettinje," replied Hal, "where you shall be turned over to the Montenegrin authorities to meet the fate you deserve!"

CHAPTER X

FLIGHT

Nicolas stopped short in his tracks. His face went red, then white, then flushed a dull red again. For a moment there was a deathly silence and then the Montenegrin sprang toward Hal with a cry of fury. The boy stood his ground.

"I wouldn't if I were you," he said very quietly.

His automatic glistened in his hand at his hip. Nicolas gazed down and then pulled himself up short as his eyes rested on the weapon. He said nothing.

"I'm glad to see you're sensible," Hal continued. "Now you will take the lead, and for your own sake, I advise you to take the shortest cut in the general direction of Cettinje. Ivan, and you, Nikol, will see that he goes in the proper direction."

The dwarf's face was covered by a comical grin and his long arms waved about eagerly as he gave his assent. He turned to Stubbs.

"You will walk with me?" he asked.

For a moment Stubbs hesitated. He gazed first at the little

Clair W. Hayes

man and then at the great bulk of Nicolas. Then his eyes roved to the huge form of Ivan.

"By Jove! I'd rather be alongside Ivan there," he muttered to himself, "but it wouldn't do to let this little fellow think I'm afraid. You're taking a long chance, Anthony, but I guess you had better do it. All right," he said to Nikol, and ranged himself at the dwarf's side.

"I wouldn't try any tricks if I were you, Nicolas," said Ivan, as he swung into step behind the traitor, Nickol and Stubbs, the prisoner in the center.

Colonel Edwards and Colonel Anderson came next in line and Hal and Chester brought up the rear.

"It's a good two days' journey back," said Hal to Chester, "and, the chances are, we will encounter many of Nicolas' friends en route. We'll have to be careful."

"We shall indeed," returned his chum. "One little slip and there is no telling what may happen."

Night brought them to Ivan's cavern again and there they decided to spend the night. It had now been more than twenty-four hours since they had closed their eyes and all were tired out.

They experienced no difficulty getting Nicolas under the rock into the cavern, nor did the Montenegrin seek to attack them as they crawled after him, as Hal had half feared he would. He seemed completely dejected and downcast. He had not spoken a word during the day's march.

"I'll put him in your erstwhile prison," Ivan said to Chester with a grin. "I guess he'll be safe enough there for the night."

He did so.

"Well, I'm going to turn in," said Stubbs. "I'm dead for sleep. I tell you, it's no fun hoofing it over these mountains, particularly when you are guarding a prisoner like I have been all day, never knowing what minute he may make a break for liberty. No, sir, it's no fun."

"Did you watch him pretty closely, Stubbs?" asked Chester.

"I did," replied Stubbs, briefly.

"Why?" continued Chester. "Afraid he might jump you? Hope you didn't think he could catch you if you had a two-foot start."

Stubbs drew himself up majestically.

"What do you mean by that?" he demanded in a ruffled tone.

"Oh, nothing," said Chester, smiling.

"If you mean to insinuate that I was afraid—" began Stubbs in an injured tone.

"What!" interrupted Chester. "You afraid, Mr. Stubbs? You do me an injustice, I assure you. Why, I have seen you fight, Mr. Stubbs. Now, do you, by any chance, remember your battle with three wildcats?"

"I do," said Stubbs, considerably pleased. He turned to Nikol. "Did I ever tell you about that fight?" he asked.

Nikol shook his head and eyed the little war correspondent with interest.

Clair W. Hayes

"Well, I did," continued Stubbs. "It was in Belgium. Three of the beasts attacked me in the dark and gave me a terrific struggle. But I killed them all, as these two boys can tell you."

Nikol was all smiles. He was glad that the man who had conquered him was such a royal gladiator.

"And you were not hurt?" he asked.

"Oh, nothing to speak of," said Stubbs, modestly. "A few scratches. Nothing serious."

"They are bad beasts to fool with," said Nikol. "My brother had both eyes scratched out in an encounter with a single wildcat. And you killed three."

"There wasn't much chance of your eyes being scratched out, was there, Mr. Stubbs?" said Chester.

"And why not?" demanded the little man,

"Come now, Mr. Stubbs," said Chester, "you don't mean to tell me you have forgotten you were lying flat on your face dodging bullets when the cats jumped you."

"No, I hadn't forgotten," said Stubbs in an injured tone. "But was it my fault that I had stumbled over a stone in the darkness a moment before?"

"Well, no, possibly not," Chester admitted. "But it's funny you didn't think to mention that stone at the time."

"If you are determined to laugh at me," said Stubbs with an air of ruffled dignity, "I have nothing more to say. Any man is likely to fall."

"So he is, Mr. Stubbs," agreed Chester, "and I don't know but I'd fall myself if I saw three wildcats coming for me. Yes, I would, and I'd try to get my head just as deep in the ground as possible, like an ostrich, and then maybe they couldn't see me."

For a moment Mr. Stubbs glared at the lad angrily and seemed about to speak; then turned on his heel angrily and strode to the far side of the cavern, where was the pallet which had been assigned to him.

Chester broke into a little laugh, which died suddenly as he stared down into the angry face of Nikol, which glared up at him.

There was a deep frown on the dwarf's face and he tapped himself upon the breast with one finger as he said:

"Any man who insults my friend, insults me. You have cast reflections upon my friend's courage. He, being your friend, overlooks it; but I, the man whom he worsted in fair fight, cannot. You must apologize."

Here Hal interfered. He had had such an encounter with the dwarf himself and he understood the situation.

"Hey, Stubbs!" he called. "Come back here, quick!"

Stubbs, just about to lie down upon his pallet, hurried back. He took in the situation at a glance and turned upon Nikol angrily.

"Here," he cried. "You keep out of my quarrels. I was big enough to attend to you, I can do the same with the rest of them."

"But he said—" protested the dwarf, pointing a finger at Chester.

"I don't care what he said," Stubbs said. "I can fight my own battles."

Nikol, deeply offended, drew back, and without another word, walked to the pallet that had been assigned to him. Stubbs, feeling somewhat better now that he had been able to berate some one and thus soothe his injured feelings, also stalked away without another word and lay down on his pallet. A moment later he was fast asleep.

"Do you suppose there is need for one of us to stand watch, Ivan?" asked Hal.

"I do not believe so," was the reply. "No one knows where my cavern is and we are not likely to be disturbed."

"I vote we turn in immediately then," said Colonel Edwards.

"Second the motion," said Colonel Anderson. "We've got to be on the move early and we've got to have some sleep first."

"Here goes, then," said Chester, and moved to his own place.

The others also sought their pallets and soon there was silence in the cavern. Completely worn out, the travelers slept like logs.

Several hours later, had they not been so completely exhausted, the sleepers undoubtedly would have heard strange noises from that part of the cavern in which Nicolas had been confined.

Came a faint grinding sound, which gradually became louder

and louder, but which, after a time, ceased altogether. Then came a softer sound, that of footsteps coming slowly from the dark passageway; and a moment later Nicolas himself stepped into the glare of the fire.

His clothing was torn about the shoulders and his open hands dripped little drops of blood. He rubbed them together tenderly.

"Had I been a weaker man it would have been impossible," he muttered.

For he had pushed aside the heavy rock that guarded his prison—a rock that Ivan had believed not another man save himself could move. Apparently Nicolas had been under-estimated.

Now the Montenegrin moved softly toward the entrance to the cave, fearful at every step that he would awaken the sleepers. It was dark within and this fact probably is all that prevented his escape.

In moving toward the entrance he passed close to the pallet upon which Stubbs slept. One of the little man's hands was stretched out across the floor and Nicolas' heavy boot came down squarely upon it.

A sudden loud cry shattered the deathly stillness of the night, followed by a more piercing cry.

Instantly every one was awake, though only half so, for the awakening had come so suddenly.

At Stubbs' first outcry, Nicolas, with a muttered imprecation, had dashed for the exit. He fell upon his knees and was about to crawl outside when Nikol, more wide awake than the others, flung himself forward and clasped his long arms about the Montenegrin's neck.

Nicolas drew back in the cave and pulled himself to his feet in spite of the dwarf's frantic efforts to hold him down. Then, seeing the size of his opponent, Nicolas laughed aloud and sought to fling the little man from him. But Nikol held him firmly.

But in spite of the dwarf's great strength, Nicolas was too big and powerful for him. The powerfulness the dwarf might have overcome, but the size was too much.

Plucking away the arms that were tightened about his neck, Nicolas held the dwarf away from him with his left hand, then struck him heavily in the face with his right. Taking a step more toward the center of the cavern, he hurled his opponent across the room.

Nikol struck the floor with a thud and lay still.

Now, realizing the need of haste, Nicolas turned quickly and made as though to move toward the exit. But he had delayed too long. The dwarf's efforts to hold him, though futile, had been enough to prevent the Montenegrin's escape.

A second huge form—the form of Ivan—barred the exit.

"Come on, have a try," said Ivan, with a grin.

Nicolas gave a loud cry—the cry of a cornered beast. Then he sprang.

"I'll kill you!" he yelled in a voice of thunder.

CHAPTER XI

A FIGHT

All the others in the cavern were on their feet now, all save Nikol, who still lay unconscious where Nicolas had hurled him. Stubbs shrank back in the dark, but Hal, Chester and the two British officers quickly produced revolvers with which they covered Nicolas.

Ivan, out of the tail of his eye, caught sight of these movements. He let out a roar even as Nicolas sprang upon him.

"Put up those guns!" he shouted. "I'll attend to this fellow with my bare hands. Stand back!"

There was something in the voice of the big Cossack that impelled the others to obey; and they drew back, circling about to watch the struggle. Even Stubbs picked up courage enough to come forward; and hardly had the fight begun when Nikol, too, pulled himself up and cast his eyes upon the combatants.

Nicolas sprang upon Ivan with outstretched arms, his fingers spread wide. His object was to clasp one of his strong hands about Ivan's throat, thus obtaining an advantage at the outset.

Clair W. Hayes

But Ivan had divined his intention at the moment he sprang, and ducking with remarkable agility for a man of his size, he came up inside the other's arms and grasped his opponent around the middle with both arms.

Then he squeezed; and the spectators drew their breaths audibly, for it seemed that no man could stand such a strain. But Nicolas bore up under it, and when Ivan, out of wind, was forced to relinquish his hold, Nicolas whirled upon him quickly and the fingers of his left hand sank into the Cossack's throat. Chester uttered a faint cry of alarm, for a hold such as this, obtained by such a powerful man as Nicolas, was indeed a thing to be feared. Ivan leaped quickly backward, carrying Nicolas with him, but the latter retained his hold; and then he brought his right fist up under Ivan's chin. It was a hard blow and Ivan staggered.

With his left hand, Nicolas jerked the big Cossack forward again, and shot his right fist into Ivan's face as he did so. Then, apparently thinking his opponent done for, he released his grip on Ivan's throat and stepped back.

But he had counted without the endurance and courage of the giant Cossack. The fingers about his throat gone, Ivan, his head reeling dizzily from the effects of the hold and the two hard blows, staggered back several paces; then, with a loud cry, sprang forward again.

Nicolas also cried aloud as he stepped forward to meet the antagonist he considered all but beaten. Ivan came forward with arms outstretched, and unheeding the two hard blows that Nicolas struck him, he again grasped the Montenegrin in a tight embrace. Nicolas wrapped his arms about Ivan; and there they stood for the space of several seconds, each vainly trying to move the other.

Suddenly Ivan gave back a step and as Nicolas came forward with him, the Cossack thrust a leg behind his opponent and pushed with all his might. Nicolas was caught off his balance and before he could recover himself Ivan twisted sharply with his leg. Nicolas went over backwards, with Ivan on top of him.

The two men struck the floor with a terrible crash; a cry was wrung from the spectators, for it seemed that a fall with such force could mean nothing less than broken bones for one of the fighters. But apparently it did not; for, still locked in each other's embrace, the men were struggling furiously for advantage upon the floor.

Ivan was still on top, but the Montenegrin, with both arms around the Cossack's neck, was making desperate efforts to roll his opponent over.

Nicolas lay squarely upon his back and Ivan's arms, wrapped around him at the moment of encounter, were pinioned beneath the other. The big Cossack was making strenuous attempts to free his right hand and still hold his opponent down with his great bulk. And at last he succeeded.

At the same moment Nicolas also released his hold and flopped over on his face. Apparently he had given up all hope of overcoming Ivan and was now acting purely upon the defensive. Ivan acted too late to prevent his opponent from turning over, but now he seized him by both shoulders, and planting his feet firmly upon the ground, by a mighty effort, jerked Nicolas to his feet.

It was a marvelous exhibition of strength and brought a cry from Stubbs, than whom there was no more interested spectator of the struggle. Nicolas now whirled suddenly and his right fist caught Ivan a terrible and unexpected jolt on the

Clair W. Hayes

point of the chin. Ivan reeled back several paces and Nicolas followed him closely, shouting:

"I've got you!"

The words seemed to have a strange effect upon Ivan. He seemed to recover himself with an effort and his right and left fists shot almost simultaneously in mighty blows. The first went wild, but the second caught Nicolas squarely upon the side of the neck and checked his rush. Before he could give ground, Ivan brought his huge right fist forward again to the point of Nicolas' chin. The Montenegrin reeled.

But Ivan, having the advantage for really the first time, gave his man no time to recover. He leaped forward and for a third time seized his opponent in a close embrace. This time Nicolas had been unable to draw a deep breath before the great arms closed about him and he weakened suddenly.

In fact, he weakened so suddenly, that Ivan, believing victory his, released his hold; and this overconfidence almost proved the Cossack's undoing. Nicolas, realizing that he could not again free himself from Ivan's embrace, had decided upon a bold stroke, and by apparently giving up the struggle had placed himself in Ivan's power absolutely.

Then, when Ivan released his hold, Nicolas dropped suddenly to his knees and seized Ivan by the legs and pulled sharply. Caught completely off his guard, Ivan toppled over backwards. Nicolas jumped upon the prostrate form and again his fingers sought Ivan's throat.

But Ivan was too quick for him and the fingers failed to find their mark. Ivan doubled up his knees suddenly and thus prevented Nicolas from obtaining his hold; then, straightening out his legs, he hurled Nicolas from him. Instantly the

Cossack was on his feet and after his opponent.

Nicolas also sprang to his feet and as the two men came together again they threw wrestling tactics to the winds and brought their fists into play. It was plainly apparent that neither had ever been schooled in the art of self-defense and there was nothing skillful about the fight that followed.

The attempts of each to ward off the blows of the other were ludicrous and of little avail. Almost every blow started went home and it became apparent to the spectators that in this kind of fighting the man who could withstand the most punishment and land the hardest blows must be the victor.

Several hard jolts had found their way to Ivan's face, but he did not show any symptoms of being unable to continue the battle. His face was a sight, but so was the face of Nicolas, for the matter of that. Both men swung hard and often, and nine out of every ten times each landed.

Also both were panting heavily now and it was perfectly plain that the fight must come to an end soon. And it did, but more suddenly than could have been expected.

Nicolas, swinging wildly for Ivan's chin, had left an opening as large as a house. The merest novice must have taken advantage of it. To Hal and Chester, both skillful boxers, it was the best opening that had been presented during the entire fight, and Hal cried out:

"Quick, Ivan!"

But his words were not needed. Ivan had seen the opening and had acted promptly.

"Smack!" his right fist landed heavily between Nicolas' eyes.

Clair W. Hayes

"Smack!" it was his left landing on the point of Nicolas' jaw.

"Crash!" It sounded like the breaking of bones. There was a brief silence, followed by another crash. The first was Ivan's right over Nicolas' mouth and the second was the sound caused as Nicolas tumbled to the ground, unconscious.

There was a twinkle in Ivan's eye as he surveyed his fallen foe.

"Some fighter, that fellow," he said. "I didn't believe he had it in him. But I would have had him sooner if he hadn't fooled me."

"You certainly would," said Hal. "You see, Ivan, that's your trouble. You know nothing of boxing. Had you been, a boxer you could have polished him off easily."

"There is no science to using your fists," said Ivan decidedly. "The only thing is to hit your opponent before he hits you."

"True enough," said Chester, "and that's where skill plays a part. For instance now, I suppose I could keep you from ever touching me, big as you are, and I venture to say I could land upon you almost at will, though possibly not hard enough to put you out. You're too big for that."

"Ho! Ho!" laughed Ivan gleefully. "Hear the little fellow talk. Why, you couldn't even lay a finger on me. I would just hold out one of my long arms and you couldn't get near me."

Chester smiled.

"It sounds easy enough," he said. "But take my word for it, I know what I am talking about."

"Well, show me," said Ivan.

"I will some time," was the reply. "Right now we'll have to tie Nicolas up and finish our sleep."

But when Nicolas had been safely secured, Ivan declared that he would not go to sleep until he had proven to Chester just how easy it would be to handle him.

"Well, all right, then," said Chester, "I'll show you. But remember, don't you crack me too hard if you do happen to land."

Chester placed himself quickly in an attitude of defense, left arm extended slightly, right arm well back. Crouching slightly and treading on his toes, he stepped lightly around Ivan, who, with arms wide, waited for him to come in.

Chester feinted quickly with his left and brought his right forward as he stepped in close. The right fist bumped the giant's chin gently, for Chester had not struck hard. A moment later his left landed almost in the same spot, a trifle harder, and he escaped Ivan's rush and wild swing by side-stepping nimbly.

There was a puzzled expression on Ivan's face as he followed the lad about the cavern, Chester dancing nimbly first to this side and then that. Once the lad let the giant come close, and when he swung, Chester jerked his head aside sharply and the blow passed over his shoulder.

Quickly then Chester stepped forward and with his open left palm smacked Ivan smartly across the left cheek. He performed a similar operation with his right; then stepped back and dropped his hands.

Clair W. Hayes

"Well?" he said, eying Ivan inquiringly.

"Well, you did it," said Ivan, greatly crestfallen. "How, I don't know. Will you teach me?"

"Some time," said Chester. "Now, let's finish that sleep."

CHAPTER XII

A CHASE

"We ought to be pretty close to the place we left our horses," said Chester.

"I was just thinking that, myself," agreed Colonel Anderson. "Must be around here some place."

"We shall be there within the hour," said Nikol, to whom the situation had been explained. He had declared he could lead them straight to the place they had left the animals.

"So you see, Mr. Stubbs, we are not coming back in such a hurry after all," said Hal.

"We're not there yet," mumbled Stubbs. "An hour is an hour. We've been altogether too lucky, if you ask me. It's about time something happened."

"Croaking again, eh?" said Chester. "I never saw a fellow like you before. You see trouble in everything."

"So I do—when I'm with you," declared Stubbs. "It's been my experience that wherever you and Hal happen to be, there also is trouble. I'm a peaceable man, I am. I believe in taking all precautions. But here we go, walking along as though we were on your uncle's farm. No thought of danger among any of you. But I've got a hunch—"

"You've always got a hunch," Hal interrupted.

"Well, all right," said Stubbs. "Just remember I've warned you."

They continued on their way in silence.

"To tell the truth, we have been remarkably fortunate," declared Colonel Edwards. "I had expected to bump into some of Nicolas' friends before this. It's funny."

"It's not too late yet," said Stubbs.

"Mr. Stubbs," said Chester, with some exasperation, "if you—"

"Hold on," said Stubbs. He pointed ahead and slightly to the left. "Here comes a gang after us now."

The others glanced in the direction indicated. A body of men afoot, perhaps a dozen all told, were approaching.

"Yes," said Chester, "here comes a gang, but that's no sign they are enemies."

"Everybody is an enemy in these parts," said Stubbs sententiously.

"By George, you are the limit, Stubbs!" declared Chester. "Now, I'll tell you what I'll do. I'll just bet you something pretty you're wrong in this case."

"Well, I ain't wrong,' returned Stubbs, forgetting his

grammar. "I'll take that bet. But in the meantime you fellows have a look at your guns. I may need protection."

This was good advice and the others realized it. They acted on it and the chamber of Colonel Anderson's revolver snapped with a click that emphasized his next remark:

"Can't trust them," he said.

The men were close now, and they appeared to be friendly enough. At sight of the prisoner in the center, one of them cried:

"Ho, Nicolas! where are you going?"

Quickly Hal stepped behind the prisoner and out of sight of the strangers, his revolver was pressed into Nicolas' back.

"No foolishness," he said in a low voice.

"Rather risky for you in these parts, isn't it, Nicolas?" said another of the strangers.

Nicolas heeded Hal's advice.

"I'm with friends," he returned. "There are enough of us here to look out for ourselves."

"Where are you bound?"

"Not far. I have a little business a couple of miles farther on."

"Want any company?"

Nicolas hesitated a moment and there came a queer gleam into his eye. And before Hal could say a word, he replied:

"Well, you can come along if you want to."

This reply staggered the others a bit, but it was too late now. Hal saw that he had not acted promptly enough, but to order Nicolas to change his decision would have aroused the suspicion of the others. There was nothing for it but to make the best of a bad situation.

"All right, we'll come along then, Nicolas," said the man who appeared to be the leader of the newcomers. "Might be a little gold in it for us, eh?"

"There might be," agreed Nicolas, with an evil smile.

Hal held a whispered consultation with the others and it was agreed it would be foolish to bring matters to a climax now.

"Wait until we get our horses," was Chester's advice.

The augmented party now continued on its way.

Half an hour later they came to the place where they had left their horses some days before. The man who had taken care of them advanced to meet the party.

"Horses still here?' asked Colonel Edwards.

The man nodded.

"And can you spare us three extra ones?"

The man considered.

"Do you wish to buy?" he asked at last.

Colonel Edwards indicated that he did.

"Then I can accommodate you," was the reply. "I have a dozen of my own animals, but times are hard and I need the money."

He named a sum and Colonel Edwards agreed to pay it.

"Have them all brought out immediately," the Colonel instructed.

The man bowed and departed after pocketing the money the Colonel gave him. Colonel Edwards returned to the others.

"It's all right," he said in a low voice. "Our horses are still here and I have bought three more—one each for Nikol, Ivan and Nicolas."

"Good," said Hal.

He gathered his friends about him, Nicolas in the center, and in a few brief words explained a plan he had hit upon:

"We'll walk slowly toward the barn," he said. "Nicolas will tell the others to remain where they are." He eyed the traitor coldly. "Then we'll dash into the barn and mount. When we are all ready, we'll make a dash for it, shooting as we do so."

"As good a plan as any, I guess," said Colonel Edwards, after a moment's hesitation. "Let's get started."

Slowly they moved toward the barn. Nicolas' friends, seeing him moving away, followed, but still kept at some distance.

The friends entered the barn without being molested. The mountaineer had just finished with the last horse and Hal gave the word for all to mount.

Clair W. Hayes

"Keep Nicolas in the center," he said, "and if he makes a false move, shoot him. He's too dangerous a man to be running around loose."

While the others mounted, Hal moved to the door to watch the men without. He arrived there just in time to meet a man who would have entered. Hal produced his automatic.

"Get back there!" he commanded.

The man took one look at the revolver and leaped back in a hurry. A moment later a voice called:

"What's the matter in there, Nicolas?"

"Answer him," said Chester, prodding Nicolas with his revolver. "Tell him everything is all right."

Nicolas did so.

Came the voice from without again:

"Trying to give us the slip, eh? Don't want to divide up the gold with us, I guess? Well, we're coming in after you."

"All ready?" asked Hal at this juncture.

Chester glanced around quickly.

"Ready, as soon as you mount," he replied quietly. "Hurry!"

Hal took one more look out the door and saw that the men were approaching, separated widely.

"They're coming!" he cried, and leaped astride his horse. Then he called to the mountaineer,

"Open the door wide!"

For a moment the mountaineer hesitated. He saw that there was trouble coming and he knew that it was none of his business.

Hal aimed his automatic at him.

"Open it wide, quick!" he commanded.

The man hesitated no longer. He threw wide the door.

Again Hal glanced quickly about him; then gave the command in a sharp voice:

"Forward!"

Out the door they charged at a gallop—Hal and Chester in the lead, next Colonel Anderson and Nicole, then Nicolas and Stubbs, with Ivan and Colonel Edwards bringing up the rear.

Outside the door the enemy had drawn somewhat closer together and they stood with drawn revolvers as the riders charged.

There was no time for flight, and in spite of the fact that the charge was a distinct surprise, the foe opened with their revolvers.

Without checking their wild speed, Hal and Chester fired point blank into the faces of the men who barred their way. Whether they hit or not it was impossible to tell, but two men who were unable to jump out of the way in time, were knocked down by the foremost horses and the rest of the little troop passed over their prostrate forms.

Clair W. Hayes

But now beyond the enemy, Hal and Chester, leading, did not check the speed of their horses, for Colonel Edwards had mentioned the fact that there were more horses in the barn, and all knew that there would be pursuit.

Behind, some of the men had fallen to their knees and taken deliberate aim at the flying riders, and the sharp crack, crack of the weapons continued for several seconds. Bullets flew near, but not one struck home.

Out of revolver shot, Hal and Chester drew up their horses to take stock.

"Any one hit?" demanded Hal.

There was no reply.

"All right," said Hal, "we'll move on again."

Colonel Edwards, glancing to the rear at that moment, called:

"Here they come!"

The others looked back.

It was true. With loud shouts and waving their revolvers aloft, almost a dozen men galloped forward.

There came a cry of alarm from Stubbs, in the center of the little troop.

"Hey! Let's get away from here."

He dug his heels into his horse's ribs and dashed through the others.

"Spread out!" ordered Hal. "We make too good a mark this way."

The others obeyed this order, Ivan still keeping close behind Nicolas, and then Hal commanded:

"Forward!"

They went forward at a rapid gallop. The pursuers gave chase with wild yells, firing wildly as they did so.

CHAPTER XIII

A SAD LOSS

The leader of the flight was Anthony Stubbs. He had covered considerable distance when the others started and was now well in advance. The little man's heels continued to dig at the ribs of the horse he bestrode, and the animal, snorting and with ears laid back, covered the ground in great bounds.

Hal and Chester, riding close to each other, kept an eye on the others; and after they had ridden perhaps half a mile, they perceived that Nicolas and Ivan were lagging behind.

"Nicolas is holding back!" shouted Chester.

Hal shook his head.

"His weight is too great for the horse," Hal shouted back. "Same with Ivan."

This was plainly true and the lads saw that the pursuers were gaining on them.

Hal headed his horse diagonally across the road and slowed down a bit. Chester followed suit. Perceiving this movement, the others also checked the speed of their horses, all save

Stubbs, who was now far ahead.

As Nicolas came abreast of Hal he suddenly leaned over his horse, and before the lad could realize what was up, he seized Hal's revolver, which was in a holster at his side. Hal grabbed for it too late.

With an evil light in his eye, the Montenegrin leveled the revolver directly at Hal and his finger tightened on the trigger. But another brain had acted more quickly than Nicolas'.

Two sharp reports came almost together. Hal felt a bullet brush past his ear. Nicolas dropped suddenly from his horse. Turning, Hal gazed into the calm face of Nikol and in the dwarf's hand was a smoking revolver. He had whipped out his revolver and fired in the nick of time.

Hal realized that he owed his life to the dwarf and he smiled at him slightly.

A quick look at the prostrate form of Nicolas showed that he was beyond human aid, and Hal also realized the need of haste, as the pursuers were even now within range and bullets whined about the fugitives.

"Forward!" he cried.

Again they set off at a gallop.

Ten minutes later Hal again noticed that Ivan was lagging behind. He drew his horse down until Ivan came up with him. A moment later Colonel Edwards also dropped back on even terms with them.

"Go ahead. Don't wait for me," shouted Ivan.

Hal shook his head slightly, as did Colonel Edwards.

"I tell you, it's no use," said Ivan. "This horse can't carry me much farther. Ride on!"

The others paid no heed.

Suddenly Ivan drew rein, pulling his horse back on his haunches, and leaped lightly to the ground. Then, before the others realized his intention, he drew his revolvers and faced the pursuers.

Quickly Hal and Colonel Edwards checked their horses, wheeled about and hurried back to him.

"You are fools!" said Ivan hoarsely. "There is no need for all of us to die. I could have held them off until the rest of you were safe. It is not too late yet. Ride on!"

For answer Hal leaped lightly to the ground and Colonel Edwards followed suit. The latter produced two revolvers and Hal one, for his other still lay beside the body of Nicolas.

"Into the woods here, quick!" Hal commanded.

The others obeyed him; and they moved from their perilous positions not a moment too soon, for the pursuers had found the range and revolver bullets whistled about them as they darted for shelter.

Ahead, Chester now discovered that the others had stopped. He checked his own horse, and calling to Colonel Anderson and Nikol, wheeled about and dashed down the road, the others following.

Chester allowed the reins to fall loose on his horse's neck and in each hand glistened a revolver. Colonel Anderson and Nikol were also prepared.

Some distance beyond where Hal, Colonel Edwards and Ivan had dismounted, the pursuers had drawn rein; and now Chester, Colonel Anderson and Nikol charged right at them.

In spite of their numbers, the pursuers, after one hasty volley, turned and fled as the three charged down upon them. The three fired once each at the foe and one man dropped. Then they checked their horses, dismounted and made their way into the woods, where they joined the others.

"Well," said Chester. "Here we are. Now what?"

"I don't know," said Hal. "We might push on through the woods, leaving the horses here, or we might wait until dark and make another break. We can probably lose our pursuers some way."

"I should say the latter is the better plan," said Colonel Edwards. "If Ivan will start first, we can come on an hour later. We can protect his flight. Because of his great weight his horse cannot keep up with the rest of us."

Ivan protested. He didn't want to go and leave the others behind. But at last he agreed.

"Then I can see no reason for waiting until dark," said Chester. "Let Ivan mount now and make a break for it. We can cover him. They won't get by us. An hour later we can start."

After some further discussion, this plan was adopted; and grumbling somewhat, Ivan mounted in the shelter of the

Clair W. Hayes

trees. When the Cossack was ready, Hal peered out. A short distance back he could see the pursuers and his appearance drew a shot. But the men were too far away to aim with any degree of accuracy and the shot went wild.

"All right, Ivan," the lad said. "Go!"

The big Cossack dug his heels into his horse's ribs and with a shout dashed out into the road.

There was an answering shout from behind and the thundering of horses' hoofs told those among the trees that the enemy was on the advance.

"We'll have to stop 'em!" cried Hal. "Aim carefully now."

They waited until the riders were close and then stepped into the open.

"Crack! Crack! Crack! Crack!"

The revolvers of the six friends spoke as one. Two of the approaching horsemen reeled in their saddles, then toppled to the ground. Two more dropped their weapons and uttered loud cries. The pursuers beat a hasty retreat.

"Guess that will give Ivan a chance to get away," said Hal briefly. "Now, all we have to do is to wait until he has a good start."

But the mountaineers had no mind to remain idle and let the fugitives make all the plans. Even now they were in deep consultation. There were many gestures and noddings of heads. And at last the mountaineers seemed to have hit upon a plan of action.

The men split up into small groups, and leaving their horses, picketed by the side of the road, plunged in among the trees. Hal, glancing from his place of concealment at that moment, took account of the activities of the foe.

"Something up," he whispered to the others. "They probably will attempt to surprise us. We'll have to look sharp now."

"My advice," said Colonel Edwards, "is that we split up a bit, to return here at a given signal. If we all remain here, it will be simple for them to surround us. Scattered, we may catch them at a disadvantage."

"A good plan," Hal agreed. "We'll scatter a hundred yards in each direction. And the signal to return?"

"I'll whistle," said Colonel Edwards.

"Good! Let's move."

Five minutes later, in the spot where the five had been, there remained only the five horses.

With revolvers in hands, the five friends were scattered near by, eyes wide open for the first enemy to show himself.

And the first chanced to be a scant twenty yards from Chester. He came crawling along the ground, glancing furtively about. He spied Chester at the same moment the lad saw him. The two revolvers spoke almost as one.

Chester felt a slight pain in his left arm. His opponent gave a loud cry and toppled over.

"Guess he won't bother us any more," muttered the lad grimly.

He kept his eyes peeled for sign of another of the foes. And in other parts of the woods the others did likewise.

Hal saw no sign of an enemy and after the one whom he had accounted for, neither did Chester. They kept careful watch, the while awaiting the signal that was to call them back to their horses in a final dash for safety.

From their places of concealment the lads heard a shot. There was not a second. Each was greatly worried, for neither knew who had fired it or whether friend or foe had been hit. All they could do was wait.

At last the whistle came, the signal agreed upon. It came so faintly as to be scarcely audible to those who had been awaiting it. Hal and Chester moved toward the spot where stood the horses. There they saw Colonel Edwards holding the bridle of his own animal. A moment later Colonel Anderson and Nikol appeared.

"All right. No use waiting longer," said Colonel Edwards. "Mount and we'll run for it!"

All suited the action to the word.

"Go!" commanded Colonel Edwards.

There was a strange catch in the colonel's voice and Hal glanced at him sharply before touching his horse. He saw Colonel Edwards reel suddenly in his saddle, then fall heavily to the ground.

With a cry to the others, Hal leaped quickly to the ground, ran to the fallen figure of the colonel and bent over him anxiously.

The others, at Hal's cry, also dismounted and returned to the fallen man.

"Stand guard there till I see what's wrong!" Hal commanded.

Colonel Anderson, Chester and Nikol stood with drawn revolvers.

Gently Hal lifted Colonel Edwards' head to his knee. The eyes were closed. The lad put a hand over the officer's heart. There was a faint beating.

A moment later Colonel Edwards opened his eyes. He smiled feebly.

"Guess I'm done for," he said quietly.

Hal did not reply, for the little wound just above the heart showed where the bullet had gone home.

Now Colonel Anderson knelt down beside his old friend.

"What's the matter, old man?" he said. "Did they get you?"

"They got me," replied Colonel Edwards. "You fellows go on. You can do nothing for me. It's too late."

A sudden shudder shook him and he burst into a fit of coughing. His eyes closed, but he reached forth a hand and his fingers clasped Colonel Anderson's hand.

"Tell the folks at home—" he said feebly, then became still.

Quickly Colonel Anderson placed a hand over the other's heart. Then he looked at Hal.

"Dead!" he said simply.

For long minutes all stood there silently, their hats off. How long they would have remained, it is hard to tell, but the sound of a shot close at hand awakened them to their own danger.

"We can do no good here," said Colonel Anderson quietly. "We may as well go."

"First," said Hal, "we shall move his body to a little hole in the ground I saw back here. We'll cover him up and then we'll go."

Under the very revolvers of the enemy this was done; and the four returned to their horses.

"Mount!" ordered Colonel Anderson.

The order was obeyed. Colonel Anderson gazed lingeringly toward the spot where lay the body of Colonel Edwards, and there were tears in his eyes as he did so. He drew a hand sharply across his eyes, shook himself a bit and commanded:

"Forward!"

CHAPTER XIV

SAFE

Away they went at a gallop, only four of them now. The horses, once upon the road again, let themselves out nobly and sped on like the wind. There was a single volley from the foe as the four came into the open, but all the bullets went wild, and before a second could be fired they were out of range.

Then the pursuers hurried for their own horses, mounted and again gave chase.

But if the ranks of the pursued had been thinned, so had those of the pursuers. Back in the woods lay four bodies cold in death. Of the survivors who still pursued there were seven.

The horses ridden by the four friends had benefited by the brief rest and were in condition for a long run; and all might have gone well had it not been for an unlooked-for occurrence.

As they were dashing swiftly along, Chester's horse stumbled and emitted a groan. Instantly the lad checked the animal, jumped to the ground and ran to its head. There was a look of pain in the horse's eyes and he held up one foot. Chester glanced down.

"He can't go on," the lad said; "the leg is broken."

He drew his revolver.

"Here! What are you going to do?" demanded Colonel Anderson.

"Shoot him," replied Chester quietly. "Put him out of his misery."

"Wait a moment," said the colonel, dismounting. "I know something about horses. Maybe it's not as bad as all that."

He examined the leg carefully. When he straightened up he looked at Chester and nodded.

"It's the best way," he said quietly. "There is nothing that can be done for him."

Chester stroked the horse's head gently and the animal whinnied in pain.

"I'm awfully sorry, old fellow," said the lad, "but it will be best for you."

The horse seemed to understand. Chester took aim and fired quickly.

"And now what are we going to do?" he asked.

"Climb up behind me," said Hal. "We've got a pretty fair start. May be they will not overtake us."

Chester did as Hal suggested, and the party moved on again,

but more slowly now.

It was perhaps half an hour later, when hoofbeats were heard behind.

"Here they come!" cried Hal, and dug his heels into his horse's side.

The animal responded nobly, but five minutes later it became apparent that they would be unable to distance their pursuers at this speed. The hoofbeats became plainer.

Hal drew rein.

"Dismount!" he cried.

His command was obeyed instantly.

Taking his horse by the head, Hal led him in among the trees. The others followed his lead.

"When they get by, we'll go forward again," said Hal.

They waited silently.

A few moments later the pursuers flashed by, going at a rapid gallop. When they were out of sight, Hal led his horse to the road, as did the others, and all mounted.

"We'll follow them," said the lad. "We'll have to keep our ears open, though, for they are likely to turn almost any time."

An hour later, rounding a turn in the road, Colonel Anderson, who was in advance, checked his horse suddenly. The others also drew up sharply.

Clair W. Hayes

"What's the matter?" asked Hal.

For answer Colonel Anderson pointed down the road.

There, probably half a mile away, were their pursuers, stationary.

"What do you suppose they are waiting for?" demanded Chester.

The answer came from an unexpected source.

From beyond the pursuers arose a puff of smoke, followed by a faint report. It was the sound of a revolver.

"They've bumped into another enemy of some kind," said Chester. "Wonder how strong this new force is?"

"Can't be very strong or those fellows would be heading this way," declared Hal. "Maybe they think it's us."

"That's about the size of it," declared Colonel Anderson.

There was another puff of smoke at this moment, and one of the enemy fell.

"Bully for you, whoever you are," shouted Chester. "Say!" he added, "what's the matter with taking them in the rear? They haven't spotted us yet."

"I was thinking of that," said Colonel Anderson. "Guess it can be done all right. Will your horse carry double that far, Hal?"

"He'll have to," replied the lad grimly.

"Good. Are you ready?"

"When you give the word."

"Then charge!"

Down the road at a rapid gallop went the three horses, carrying the four friends.

Hal, Colonel Anderson and Nikol each guided their mounts with their left hands, flourishing their revolvers in the right. Chester held fast to Hal with his left and also flourished a revolver with his free hand.

Nearer and nearer they came upon their unsuspecting enemies, who still stood where they had been when first discovered. Occasionally one fired his revolver at the spot from which shots came at frequent intervals now.

"Wonder why those fellows beyond don't charge, now that they must see us coming," muttered Hal to himself.

He watched the puffs of smoke as they came at intervals, and he was suddenly struck by an idea.

"By Jove!" he shouted, to make himself heard, "I'll bet there is only one man there. That's why the shots are so far apart."

"Well, we're pretty evenly matched," said Chester. "There are only six of them in condition to fight."

"Five," said Hal suddenly, as another of the enemy pitched suddenly to the ground, a shot from beyond having struck him.

"See! they are going to charge him!" cried Chester, peering

over his friend's shoulder.

It was true. The enemy had spread out as much as the road would permit and the man who appeared to be the leader raised his hand.

"We'll have to stop that," muttered Hal.

He raised his voice in a shout, which carried plainly to the foe.

The five men wheeled about suddenly and for the first time saw they were beset in the rear as well as in front. For a moment they hesitated, then turned and charged the new arrivals.

"Keep going!" shouted Hal. "And don't miss!"

The enemy fired first, but all the shots went wild. Suddenly Nikol checked his horse, took deliberate aim and fired. A rider fell to the ground. The range was still great, but Nikol's aim was true. A second man dropped at his second bullet.

Now Colonel Anderson and Hal fired simultaneously. Another man dropped—it was impossible to tell whether Hal or Colonel Anderson had scored a hit.

The two remaining riders drew their horses upon their haunches, and headed them for the friendly protection of the trees. Hal and Colonel Anderson fired a parting shot, but they were unable to tell whether the bullets had gone home.

Chester, behind Hal, had been unable to get into the battle, Hal's figure interfering with his aim.

"Well, I don't think the two of them will bother us," said Hal.

"No," Chester agreed. "And there are two loose horses. I'm going to get one of them."

"Better make it two," said Colonel Anderson. "Our ally beyond, whoever he may be, may need one."

Chester nodded.

"He deserves one," he said. "He knocked off three of these fellows."

He secured the two horses without much trouble, mounted one and led the other.

"Now we'll have an interview with our friend," he said.

They rode forward slowly.

"Funny he doesn't come out and show himself," said Hal.

"Guess he thinks we are enemies, too," suggested Colonel Anderson. "Well—whoa, there."

He broke off suddenly and ducked his head, for a bullet had whistled just above him. He raised his voice in a shout:

"Hey!" he cried in English, forgetting just where he was, "what do you mean shooting at us? Quit it. We're friends."

"That you, Hal?" came a familiar voice.

Hal, Chester and Colonel Anderson gazed into each other's eyes almost dumbfounded.

"Well, what do you think of that?" exclaimed Hal.

There came a pleased chuckle from one member of the party, who rushed forward happily.

It was Nikol.

"Now where is he going?" demanded Chester anxiously.

"Going to greet his friend Stubbs," returned Hal. "To Nikol, Stubbs is a brave man and a grand fighter; and what has happened just now will only increase his admiration. Come on, let's go and have a look for ourselves."

"Is that you, Hal, Chester?" came Stubbs' voice again.

"Yes," Hal shouted back.

They rode forward.

Anthony Stubbs, now that he had found his friends again, came forward as fast as his queer stature would permit. He was puffing and blowing so hard by the time he reached them that he could hardly talk. Of Nikol, who stuck close to his side, eyeing him admiringly, he took no notice.

"By George! It's good to see you fellows again," declared Stubbs. "I thought my days were numbered when that gang of ruffians set upon me. I didn't want to fight, but I had to. It seems to me I got seven or eight of them."

"Well, how do you happen to be here, anyhow?" demanded Chester.

"My horse threw me and went away by himself," said Stubbs mournfully. "If I ever see him again I'll tell him about it. He might have got me killed."

Nikol now forced himself in front of Stubbs and extended a hand.

"Mr. Stubbs," he said quietly, "you are a brave and gallant man."

Stubbs was pleased. He made as though to take the hand; then thought better of it. He remembered the grip of those powerful fingers.

He shuddered.

"I know it, Nikol," he said gravely.

He put out his hand and patted the dwarf on the head.

Clair W. Hayes

CHAPTER XV

MR. STUBBS EASES HIS MIND

The remainder of the journey to Cettinje was without incident. After the defeat of the mountaineers the lads felt safe, for they were once more within the borders of Montenegro and were unlikely, they knew, to encounter other enemies.

Stubbs, when informed of the death of Colonel Edwards, was greatly grieved.

"Poor fellow," he said, and added after a pause: "There is no use talking, Hal, this is no life for any one. He's likely to be snuffed out at a moment's notice. I'm going to be careful where I go in the future."

Besides the three bags of gold he had carried when he left the Albanian mountains, Hal now had the two he had taken from the body of Colonel Edwards. The two Nicolas had carried had been left with him, for there had been no time to get them. Stubbs had held on to the two entrusted to him, and Ivan, wherever he was, had two more.

It was while speaking of the gold that Hal's thoughts turned to Ivan.

"I wonder what can have happened to him?" he said.

Chester shrugged his shoulders.

"No telling," he replied. "However, I guess he'll turn up sooner or later."

And the lad was right.

It was dark when the little party came again within the first line of Montenegrin troops. Colonel Anderson announced that he would seek an audience of King Nicholas immediately. He made his wants known to the officer of the guard, and after he had explained the situation, the officer departed to learn whether the king would see the returned travelers. He returned fifteen minutes later with the announcement that the king would receive them in his field quarters immediately.

As they started for the monarch's quarters, Stubbs and Nikol both hung back.

"Come on now, Mr. Stubbs," said Chester. "The king will be as glad to see you as any of the rest of us."

"I'm not much used to kings," Stubbs protested. "Besides, this is none of my expedition. You're the fellows he wants to see."

"Nonsense," said Hal, and struck with a sudden thought, he added: "Perhaps the king will give you an interview. It would be a good thing for the *New York Gazette*."

"By Jove! you're right there," Stubbs agreed. "I must be a great newspaper man to have overlooked a thing like that. If my boss knew it I'd get fired. I'll go along."

Clair W. Hayes

Still Nikol hung back, and it took considerable coaxing before he consented to go; and then it took Stubbs to clinch matters.

"Look here, now," he said, eyeing Nikol sternly, "I took you for a brave man. You're not afraid of a king, are you?"

Nikol shook his head negatively.

"Well, if you don't come along I'll think you are," declared Stubbs. "Look at me now. I don't care particularly about going, but I want to show King Nicholas I'm not afraid of him. Come on."

He took the dwarf by the arm and the latter moved along grumbling to himself.

The king received the party in his private quarters—a large field tent. When the party was ushered into his presence, he was attended by a single orderly. He arose at their entrance. His eyes surveyed the group quickly, and he demanded:

"Where is my friend, Colonel Edwards?"

Colonel Anderson, delegated spokesman for the party by reason of his superior rank, stepped forward and replied quietly:

"He is dead, sire."

The king took a step backward and passed a trembling hand across his brow. He was silent for some moments before replying.

"Dead! One more victim of the Kaiser's militarism. Tell me, how did he die?"

Colonel Anderson explained quietly and briefly. Then, at the king's request, he went into the details of the journey; and when he had concluded, King Nicholas expressed his deep thanks for the service each member of the party had rendered him.

"And you say Nicolas, the traitor, is dead?" he questioned.

"Yes, your majesty. Nikol here," and Colonel Anderson indicated the dwarf, "saw to that."

The king turned to Nikol. Then he commanded:

"Come here!"

Trembling, in spite of his denial that he was afraid of a king, Nikol approached. The king extended a hand, and Nikol bent one knee and put his lips to the hand.

"I thank you," said King Nicholas.

Nikol, with flushed face, muttered something unintelligible and backed slowly away.

Then the king thanked each member of the party separately. Even Stubbs seemed somewhat abashed by the king's manner.

Later Colonel Anderson mentioned the gold they had brought and it was all deposited—fifteen bags of the precious metal—before the king.

"Again I thank you," said the monarch. "You may make sure that this gold will be used where it will do the most good."

A few moments later the king signified that the audience was at an end. As they passed out he spoke a final word:

"If, at any time, there is anything I am able to do for any of you, you have but to command me."

All bowed low.

"One moment," said the king as they were about to withdraw, "have you quarters?"

"No, sire," returned Colonel Anderson.

The king spoke to the officer who attended him.

"You will see that these gentlemen are provided with suitable quarters at once," he commanded. "They are my guests."

The officer saluted and motioned the others to follow him. Outside they were turned over to a second officer, who escorted them to a tent somewhat larger than the rest.

"You will make this your quarters," said the officer. "I shall send you an orderly, and if at any time there is anything you require, you have but to mention it to him."

He saluted and departed.

Left to themselves at last, Hal, Chester and the others looked about. The tent was fitted up comfortably, almost luxuriously. There were seven or eight cots within and the tent had the appearance of having sheltered men of note.

"Style to this place, if you ask me," said Stubbs, "Makes a fellow want to turn in and sleep a bit."

"And that is just what we'll do," said Chester. "I'm tired

out myself."

"Same here," agreed Hal.

Colonel Anderson and Nikol also announced that they were ready to seek repose at any time, and after some further talk, all lay down and soon were fast asleep.

The sun was high in the heavens when Chester opened his eyes. He was up and dressed quickly. Glancing around, he saw that the others, with the exception of Stubbs, who had one eye open, were still fast asleep.

"Guess I'll take a little trip by myself," the lad muttered.

He moved toward the exit.

"Wait a minute, there," Stubbs called, hopping out of his cot. "I'll go with you."

"How's that, Mr. Stubbs?" said Chester, pausing. "Why do you arise so early? Thought you always stayed until last."

"Don't you believe it," said the little man. "I like to sleep the same as the next fellow, but when I have business on hand I attend to it first."

"Business?" repeated Chester. "And what business have you on hand this morning?"

"Got to get busy and get some news," was the reply. "I'm going to have a look about this camp, ask some questions, then do a little writing; after which I'll hunt up the official censor and the rest of the gang and see what arrangements I can make toward getting my stuff sent through."

"Then I'll go with you on your hunt," Chester decided. "Maybe I can get a few pointers. I might want to get into the newspaper business myself some day."

"Don't," said Stubbs. "Take my advice and do anything else. Look at me now, I'm a fair example. Here I've been in this business for fifteen years, and what has it got me, eh? I'll tell you. It's got me a chance to get out and get shot so that people over in the good old U.S.A. can read, with their morning cup of coffee, what is going on in this benighted land. And what do I get for it? Nothing."

"And still, the excitement," said Chester.

"Excitement?" echoed Stubbs. "Now I ask you, what do I want with excitement? I can get all the excitement I want right back in New York. This is a long way to come looking for excitement."

"Well, perhaps so," Chester admitted, "but when you get back home you will be able to tell people who want to know, more about this war than they could read in the *Gazette*."

"So I can," Stubbs agreed, "but I wouldn't if these two by four censors didn't stick to their jobs so closely."

The little man slapped on his hat and stalked from the tent, calling over his shoulder:

"Come on."

Chester followed him.

Outside, Stubbs made a straight line for the first line troops.

"If you want to find out anything, you have got to get right where it is," he declared. "I could stay back here and ask questions, but I want to see things for myself."

Chester offered no objections.

Suddenly the camp seemed to spring to life. Bugles blew shrilly, men came pouring out of the tents to form into ranks. Officers darted hither and thither, shouting hoarse commands. For a moment all seemed to be confusion, but a moment later, in response to sharp commands, all became quiet and orderly.

"Something up," said Chester.

Stubbs nodded.

"An advance, I imagine," he said. "We'll see."

He approached a gruff-looking officer of forbidding aspect and addressed him in French.

"Where to?" he asked.

"To the attack," was the reply.

At the same moment a bugle rang out. Others took it up. It was the command to advance.

CHAPTER XVI

AN ENGAGEMENT

Right, left, front and rear of where Stubbs and Chester stood the troops began to move. In front they could make out the heavy guns being dragged forward, officers dashing about and gesticulating excitedly, but order reigning in the midst of apparent confusion.

From the rear now dashed a squadron of cavalry, a handsome appearing body of men. A second squadron came into sight and disappeared ahead, to be followed a moment later by a third. Other squadrons passed in rapid succession.

Chester and Stubbs kept their positions.

Half an hour passed and still the mounted horsemen swept by. Then came the infantry. Column upon column came swinging along at a dog trot, their officers urging them on. They moved silently and swiftly, apparently all ready for the terrible business in hand.

"A handsome body of men," said Stubbs. "I have never seen better."

"And the size of them," exclaimed Chester. "Must all be over six feet."

It did seem so. Great, big, husky-looking fellows they were, strong as gorillas—heavily bearded, most of them, and warmly and snugly dressed.

"They'll make these Austrians move around some, with an even break," declared Chester.

And still the troops passed, seemingly without end.

"Must be an attack in some force," said Chester.

"Or reinforcements to check an enemy's advance," declared Stubbs.

"Well," said Chester, "if there is going to be a battle, we ought to try and see something of it."

"They'll arrest us if we go fooling around here," declared Stubbs.

Chester thought quickly.

"I'll tell you," he said at length, "you saw the orderly stationed outside our tent?"

Stubbs nodded.

"We'll go back and get him. Also we'll take Hal and Colonel Anderson. They wouldn't want to miss this."

"Don't forget my old friend Nikol," said Stubbs. "Remember he is something of a fighter, too. He'll want to have a look."

They made their way back to the tent quickly and aroused

the others. The orderly placed at their disposal, once their wants were made known, volunteered to conduct them to the front.

"I'll get an automobile," he said, and departed.

Five minutes later he was back with a big car and all climbed aboard. A moment later they were being driven rapidly toward the extreme front. There, just behind the first line troops, Hal and Chester made out that the movement was in reality a defensive one. Apparently the men rushed forward so early in the morning were reinforcements.

The troops had entrenched themselves hurriedly and were preparing to resist an attack, which, the orderly informed his charges, was expected momentarily. It appeared that the Austrians had made some slight gains the day before and the Montenegrin general staff had reason to believe the offensive would be continued to-day. Accordingly, steps had been taken to resist the invader.

As the orderly explained the situation, the battle would probably be fought along a twenty-five-mile front; and he announced that at this particular moment the party was somewhere between the center and the left wing of the Montenegrin army.

"Well, we can't see much from here," said Chester.

He gazed across the hills. Then he pointed to his right, toward a not far distant elevation, somewhat higher than the others nearby, and also somewhat closer to the Montenegrin center.

"Now, if we were up there," he said, "we might be able to see something."

The orderly seemed nonplussed.

"It is from that eminence that the king and the general staff will witness the struggle," he said, "I do not know—"

"Oh, that will be all right," said Stubbs. "The king is a good friend of ours. Why, only last night he said that if we desired anything all we had to do was to call on him. Now, taking the king at his word, what we would desire most is to be allowed to witness the battle from that eminence."

The Montenegrin officer hesitated; but only for a moment. Then he said:

"If those were the king's words, he no doubt will forgive me for leading you thither."

"Most certainly he will," declared Stubbs; "in fact, he will thank you for bringing us to him."

The officer, without further words, proceeded as desired, and ten minutes later, having left the big army automobile, they climbed the eminence and took their positions not far from where the king and the general staff stood viewing the Austrian lines through their glasses.

Even as they settled themselves as comfortably as possible, the first big gun of the enemy boomed. Other big guns from the Montenegrin lines took up the action and soon the artillery engagement became general. The air was filled with terrible din and it was next to impossible to make oneself heard above the roar of battle.

Hidden batteries in the Montenegrin lines were making their fire felt. Shielded from the enemy in front, they were also, in most cases, made invisible to the Austrian air craft that

Clair W. Hayes

continually hovered overhead, sheltered as they were in dense clumps of trees and bushes.

From the Montenegrin lines now went a small fleet of aeroplanes, seeking out the hiding places of the enemy artillery and signaling back the range to the Montenegrin gunners.

For an hour the duel of big guns continued without other action of any kind. Now and then the spectators were able to make out the effect of an enemy shell as it struck within the Montenegrin line, but they were unable to determine the result of the Montenegrin fire.

Came the sound of a bugle from the rear.

"Something up!" shouted Chester at the top of his voice.

Hal nodded but said nothing. He did not feel equal to making himself heard above the terrible roar of battle.

From the Austrian line suddenly issued a squadron of cavalry, closely followed by many other squadrons. It became apparent to the spectators that the enemy had determined to silence the Montenegrin guns, or a portion of them, at any rate, by a charge.

On they came in the very face of a hail of lead that cut great gaps in their ranks, mowing men and riders down like chaff before a storm. But as fast as the ranks were thinned, they filled up again as the Austrians continued their charge, while from their rear the great Austrian guns continued to hurl their messengers of death over their heads into the ranks of the Montenegrins beyond.

Straight for a little woods in the center of the long battle line the Austrian cavalry dashed, their intention apparently being to seek temporary shelter there before charging some other part of the Montenegrin line.

Now they were almost to the trees and it seemed that they must find shelter there. This would mean that it would be a hard task for the Montenegrins to dislodge them. They were less than a hundred yards away when there came a fresh, terrible rumble and roar.

A Montenegrin masked battery had opened with its rapid-firers. Men dropped in great heaps, but the others came on.

The Austrian officer in command, realizing that he was in a trap, took the one chance left him. With what men he had, cut off from his infantry support as he was, he must either capture that masked battery, die or surrender. The only support he had now was from his own artillery, and a moment later that, too, became silent, for the masked Montenegrin battery could not be shelled without imminent risk of shooting down Austrian as well as Montenegrin.

On came the Austrians in a desperate and spectacular charge. Of the number that had sallied forth from the Austrian trench, less than half remained when they came to the edge of the little woods. These few hurled themselves forward with the utmost bravery and abandon, and for a moment it seemed that they might reach the guns, which Hal and Chester, from the eminence, could see.

But at that moment four squadrons of Montenegrin cavalry, fresh and eager for the fray, were hurled forward. They dashed out with a yell, and the two forces met just beyond the fringe of trees.

There was a terrific shock as they came together and in a moment all was confusion. Men cursed, slashed, stabbed and

Clair W. Hayes

discharged revolvers at each other, while the horses of the opposing forces fought as well as their riders.

The Montenegrin battery had now become silent, for to have fired would have been to endanger the life of friend as well as foe. The horsemen struggled desperately, hand-to-hand.

But the force of the Austrian charge had been spent. The few who remained fought bravely, but they were no match for the fresher and more powerful Montenegrin horsemen, among the best fighters in the whole world.

Slowly the Austrians were forced back. Then they gave ground faster and faster, until finally those who were left turned their horses and fled back toward their own lines. For perhaps a hundred yards the Montenegrins pursued, then, at the call of a bugle, they halted and turned back.

A moment later the rapid-firers broke loose again, cutting great holes in the ranks of the fleeing Austrians. The latter retreated even faster than they had charged, but by the time they reached the shelter of their own lines their number had been thinned by fully three-fourths.

All the way across the field dead and wounded strewed the ground. The successful Montenegrins paused for a moment and cheered wildly; then they took stock of their own dead and wounded, for they had not escaped scot-free. The hand-to-hand struggle, though brief, had been severe while it lasted, and the Austrians fought hard and well. The Montenegrin losses, though comparatively light, had been severe.

While the cavalry action was being fought, the artillery fire had slackened perceptibly; but now the cavalry of each side—what was left of it—had returned to its own lines.

The big guns took up the duel anew with even greater vigor than before.

Clair W. Hayes

CHAPTER XVII

THE BATTLE CONTINUES

Hal, Chester and Colonel Anderson had watched the battle with the eyes of veterans; Stubbs had taken in the scene with the eye of a newspaper man in the search of news. Nikol, the dwarf, had gazed at the struggling knot of horsemen in undisguised amazement.

As the Austrians, defeated, had withdrawn, each had drawn a deep breath.

"A terrible spectacle, when you stop to think of it," said Hal slowly.

"Terrible, indeed," agreed Colonel Anderson quietly; "and yet it must go on and on until the power of the Teuton allies has been crushed out forever."

"Which it will be," said Chester quietly.

All turned their eyes to the battlefield once more.

Even from where they stood they could discern a sudden activity in the Austrian lines. The action of the big field pieces became more vigorous than before. Hal, Chester and

Colonel Anderson guessed the answer immediately, as, probably, did the officers of King Nicholas' forces.

The next Austrian move was to be a grand assault under cover of artillery fire. The problem to be solved was where it would be delivered—in the center, on the right, or on the left flank.

For a brief instant Hal turned his eyes from the battlefield to the place where King Nicholas and his staff stood. Officers were arriving and departing in haste, carrying orders to the various commanders.

The fire of the Montenegrin guns also became more violent; but it was evident that the Montenegrin staff had decided to take no action until they were confident of just where the Austrians would strike.

The noise of the cannonading was tremendous. It was like the continual roar of the loudest peal of thunder. The very ground trembled from the vibrations of the big guns.

From the Austrian trenches now poured thousands of men at the double—poured in dense masses toward the Montenegrin center, the while the Austrian artillery shelled the Montenegrin center with greater energy than at any time since the battle began.

Apparently the enemy had determined upon the Montenegrin center as the objective of its grand assault.

In the open field, a small plateau, the Austrians reformed coolly, in spite of the death-dealing fire from the Montenegrin lines. The field was packed closely with the enemy, now less than half a mile away.

Clair W. Hayes

At this distance the fire of the Montenegrin artillery was terribly effective, but the Austrian line did not waver.

Steadily forward it came; and now the Montenegrins moved to meet the attack. Apparently satisfied that there was no question that the center was to be the main objective of the enemy, the Montenegrin staff ordered the bulk of the Balkan army massed there to beat back the foe.

Regiments and brigades were hurriedly drawn from the two flanks to reinforce the center. The left wing was weakened badly.

A quarter of a mile from the first Montenegrin trench the Austrians charged fiercely. All eyes were turned to that section of the field. The shock was but a few moments away.

At that moment—almost the moment of impact—a second line of men issued from the Austrian, trenches, this time on the Montenegrin left wing. These, too, supported by artillery and strong bodies of cavalry, came forward in a charge.

It seemed the Austrian commander had outgeneraled the Montenegrins, for it did not seem possible that the Montenegrin left flank could be reinforced in time to successfully withstand the shock of the Austrian attack, and there could be no doubt now that the left flank was where the main attack would be delivered.

The assault upon the center had been a feint—nothing more. The main bodies of Austrians were to be hurled against the Montenegrin left, in an effort to turn it before reinforcements could be hurried from the right flank to support the threatened center and left.

But King Nicholas, taking matters in his own hands, acted

quickly. In spite of the protests of his officers, he ordered the reinforcements so recently massed in his center back to strengthen his left; then ordered that the center hold firm at all hazards and against all numbers.

He hurried reinforcements from his right to support his center, and having taken these precautions, he was ready to give battle.

The Austrian attacking force and the Montenegrin center had come in contact long before the king had made his other moves, but there was no doubt in Nicholas' mind that his sturdy mountaineers could hold their trenches against larger numbers of the enemy.

One, two, three times the Austrians charged the trenches in the Montenegrin center. Three times they were driven back with terrible losses. The Montenegrins, in the shelter of their trenches, fought stubbornly and tenaciously. Once the first line of Austrians succeeded in obtaining a foothold in the first trench and hand-to-hand fighting ensued.

At this style of fighting the Austrians were no match for the sturdy Balkan warriors, and they were soon forced out again.

Meanwhile the Austrian main attack had come in contact with the Montenegrin left wing. Outnumbered two to one, sometimes more, the defenders fought gallantly. But the Austrians, by the very weight of numbers, swooped down upon the defenders of the first line trenches in spite of the heavy Montenegrin artillery fire.

The Montenegrins were forced to fall back to their second line; but they contested every inch of ground and by the time they had been forced out, reinforcements began to arrive. The second line of trenches held in spite of all attempts of

　　　　　　　Clair W. Hayes

the enemy to force them.

Reinforcements continued to arrive.

The Austrian artillery had now slackened its fire perceptibly, for there was danger of mowing down its own men.

King Nicholas decided upon a bold stroke. Secure in the fact that the Austrian guns could not be used at the moment, and having every confidence in his stalwart troops, in spite of the fact that they were heavily outnumbered, King Nicholas ordered a charge.

A cheer went up along the Montenegrin line.

With bayonets fixed and every nerve tense, the Montenegrins poured suddenly from their trenches. They charged like wild men.

The advantage of the surprise was theirs—the advantage of their impetuous devotion to the cause they served; and the force of their charge was irresistible. It carried all before it.

In vain the Austrian officers tried to rally their men. The sight of these determined, grim-faced men pouring from their trenches bewildered the Austrian troops. They gave ground, slowly at first, then more swiftly; and five minutes later they were in full retreat, with the Montenegrins in close pursuit.

Once the Austrian commander succeeded in reforming his men for a stand; but the Montenegrins rushed on as though they could have carried the Rock of Gibraltar itself, and again the Austrians broke and fled.

The Montenegrins pursued them for probably a quarter of a mile, cutting them down and bayoneting them as they ran.

Then the bugle sounded a recall and the Montenegrins drew off.

It was then, too, that the great Austrian guns opened on them again, doing fearful havoc. The Montenegrins suffered greater losses on their return to their trenches than they had during the entire engagement up to that time.

In the center, the battle was still raging; but now that he had been victorious on his left, King Nicholas immediately hurled his weary men to the support of his center. Also he drew upon his already weakened right wing; for the advantage was his and he was determined to make the most of it.

The Austrians fell back in the center.

Now the Montenegrins opened with their heavy artillery, which was rushed forward to shell the retreating foe. Again King Nicholas ordered a charge along his entire front.

With the present morale among the enemy, King Nicholas decided it was time to push his advantage further. He had determined to drive the foe from its own trenches.

The Montenegrins advanced confidently all along the line, pursuing the Austrians closely in the center. Cavalry and infantry, under the protection of the giant batteries, were hurled forward and dashed upon the Austrians with ferocity.

Rapidly they covered the open distance to the first Austrian trenches and leaped into them without thought of death. The Austrians, brought to bay at last, fought desperately, but the Montenegrins, once having gained the whip hand, were not to be denied.

The fighting in the Austrian trenches continued for what

Clair W. Hayes

seemed an eternity; but finally the Austrians broke and fled.

The Montenegrins, flushed with victory, advanced again, and under cover of their artillery, stormed the enemy's second line trenches. These, too, were won after a desperate struggle and heavy losses on both sides, and with these the Montenegrins, worn and spent, rested content.

The troops were for pushing on after the Austrians, but King Nicholas called a halt.

"My brave men!" he exclaimed, with tears in his eyes. "They have done a day's work to-day that will live in memory for generations to come. It is a brilliant victory."

The duel of heavy guns continued, but the infantry fighting was over for the day. The Montenegrins, in their newly won trenches, fell to preparing them to resist the attack that they knew would come sooner or later, while the Austrians were taking account of their losses and making ready for a new assault.

Stubbs laid a hand on Chester's arm.

"Didn't I tell you they looked like real fighters?" he exclaimed.

"Certainly, I have never seen better," returned the lad.

Stubbs turned to Nikol.

"Well, Nikol," said he, "what do you think of these fellows as fighters?"

Nikol eyed him in silence for several moments. But at last he spoke.

"Mr. Stubbs," he said quietly, "they are better fighters than you or I."

　Clair W. Hayes

CHAPTER XVIII

IVAN AGAIN

"Come," said Colonel Anderson, "the battle is over. There will be no more fighting to-day. Let us move."

Slowly all made their way back toward their quarters, talking over the battle as they went.

It was late in the afternoon. The battle had raged all day, and now for the first time the friends felt the need of food. Instead of taking camp fare, to which they were invited by the Montenegrin officer who accompanied them, they decided to go to a little village not far from the camp, where the officer informed them they could get a substantial meal at a certain, little restaurant.

Thither they made their way and to their satisfaction found the information correct. Then, their appetites satisfied, they left the restaurant and started back to the camp.

It was now after dark and as they walked slowly, discussing events of the day, they came upon a knot of men engaged in some sort of an argument.

"My curiosity always gets the better of me," said Chester

"Let's have a look," and he led the way toward the gesticulating group.

It was plain, as they drew nearer, that the argument was heated. Loud voices broke the stillness of the night, and one of them, a deep bass, had a familiar ring. One look at the faces in the crowd and they recognized its owner.

It was none other than Ivan, whom they had last seen when he made his dash for liberty in the mountains.

Ivan was in the very center of the crowd, and as Hal, Chester and the others came close, in the glare of a dim light he could be seen gesticulating violently.

"I tell you," he shouted, "I have no money."

"But you showed two bags of gold in the restaurant," said one of the men pressing in on him.

"Well, what if I did?" demanded Ivan. "That gold is not mine. It belongs to your king and I am taking it to him."

"A likely story," said one man in the crowd with a sneer. "You stole it some place. We want a share."

"Oh, you do?" said Ivan, and he broke into a loud laugh. "Well, you won't get it. First, however, I want to tell you again, that I did not steal the money and that it is not mine."

"Then why," said another of the crowd, "why did you dip into one of the bags to pay for a drink at the restaurant?"

"Why?" echoed Ivan in a loud voice. "I'll tell you. Because I was dry."

"But if the gold is not yours?"

For a moment Ivan appeared somewhat flustered. But he made answer after a moment.

"I am entitled to the price of a glass of wine for carrying this gold for the king. That's why."

"It's my belief you filled up on wine before you got the gold," said another voice in the crowd.

"You may have any belief you choose," shouted Ivan angrily. "But now stand aside. I am going on my way."

"Not until you give us a share of your spoils," said a voice close to him.

"Ho!" said Ivan. "You think so. Ho! Ho!"

He took a step forward and his merriment subsided.

"Stand aside there!" he commanded sternly.

For a moment it appeared that the crowd would give before him, but a man in the back of the crowd cried:

"What! will you run from one man, a drunken man at that?"

Another, closer to the giant, reached out a hand and sought to clutch the bag of gold Ivan held in his left hand.

With a sudden movement and a loud cry, Ivan stretched forth a hand and seized the man by the throat. Then he lifted him high in the air and hurled him through space. The man struck the ground with a loud cry of pain.

At the same instant a second man struck at Ivan with a club.

With a cry of anger, Ivan reached forth and seized the club; then, whirling it about his head, brought it down on the man's skull. The man toppled over like a log.

Now Ivan began to laugh in glee.

"Ho! Ho!" he cried. "Come on and take the gold," and he brandished it aloft in his left hand. "What! Are you afraid of one man? Ho! Ho!"

The crowd gave back as Ivan moved forward.

A man from behind sprang forward and stabbed the giant between the shoulders with a thin knife.

Ivan whirled about with a terrible cry. Then, raising his recently acquired club, he dashed in among the crowd and laid about him right and left. Men went down on all sides and in a moment the others turned and fled.

One, from a distance, drew a revolver and fired. Whether the bullet came close to the giant, Hal could not tell, but he drew his own revolver, and springing forward, cried:

"That's enough of this! The next man to make a move I'll put a bullet through."

Chester, Nikol and Colonel Anderson ranged themselves by Hal's side and also produced their automatics. Seeing nothing else to do, Stubbs also joined them and flourished a revolver.

The crowd gave back.

Ivan turned upon the newcomers in surprise. Then he cried in a great voice:

"Well! Well! and where did you come from? I had made sure you had deserted me."

"No, we haven't deserted you," said Hal. "We simply missed you, that's all."

"Well, it's all right, anyhow," said Ivan. "Now come to the restaurant with me and I shall buy wine for all of us."

"Thanks, Ivan, but we don't drink wine," said Hal quietly. "If you will come with us to our quarters we will talk matters over."

"Not I, not until I have had wine," declared Ivan.

"But you have had enough wine," declared Chester.

"And how do you know I have had enough wine?" demanded Ivan, turning upon the lad.

"The way you talk makes it plain enough," replied Chester quietly. "Come, Ivan, let's get away from here."

"Well," said Ivan hesitatingly, "maybe you are right." Turning he caught sight of Nikol.

"Why, there is my old friend Nikol," he shouted. "Nikol, you will join me in a bottle of wine?"

"I shall be pleased," said Nikol, with a smile.

"Good. Come with me." He turned and made as though to move away, when suddenly his eyes lighted upon Stubbs.

"Ho! Ho!" he laughed. "And my friend Stubbs here shall accompany us."

"Thanks; some other time," said Stubbs nervously.

For answer Ivan leaned down, picked the little man up in his arms and walked away with him in spite of Stubbs' cries and struggles.

Nikol went along and for once he did not offer to take Stubbs' part.

"Great Scott! Hal, we can't stand for this," said Chester. "What shall we do?"

"Go along, I should say," said Colonel Anderson.

"But we don't drink wine," protested Hal.

"There is no reason you should. If you can get Ivan seated and talk to him he will be all right in a few minutes. Besides, he is likely to get into more trouble this way."

"I guess you're right," said Hal. "Come on, Chester."

The three followed Nikol, Ivan and the latter's struggling burden in the person of Stubbs.

They entered the restaurant right behind the others and took seats at the same table. Ivan greeted them with a smile.

"Glad to see you came along," he said. He turned to Stubbs. "What will you have?"

"Thanks, I don't drink," said Stubbs fearfully.

Clair W. Hayes

"Now, Mr. Stubbs!" said Ivan with a comical grin.

Hal now decided the affair had gone far enough.

"Listen to me, Ivan," he said quietly. "Stubbs doesn't want any wine and neither do the rest of us. You have had enough."

"And what have you to do with it?" demanded Ivan loudly.

"Just this," said Hal, and produced a revolver. "Before I'll stand for any more of this nonsense, I'll put a hole through you. Understand?"

Ivan looked at the lad, apparently bewildered, for some moments. Then he said with a laugh:

"Don't you ever shoot at me with that gun. Not ever!"

He rose to his feet and faced Hal threateningly. The lad was nonplussed. He had no idea that his bluff wouldn't work. He knew of course that he could never shoot the Cossack.

It was Chester who saved the day.

"Ivan," he said quietly. "That's not your money."

"What—what's that?" said Ivan, turning to him suddenly.

"I said that's not your money. Surely you are not a thief?"

"A thief?" cried Ivan. "Who says I am a thief?"

"I do, if you touch the money in the bag you hold there," said Chester quietly.

For a moment it seemed that the big Cossack would spring

upon Chester; but the lad stood his ground, and suddenly Ivan sank down in a chair.

"No, I'm not a thief," he mumbled. "I'm not going to be a thief."

He threw the bag of gold down heavily on the table and looked thoughtfully into space.

Chester approached him and laid a hand on his shoulder.

"There," he said calmly, "I knew you wouldn't. This, you know, is the king's money. You wouldn't touch that?"

"No," said Ivan, then added hastily: "but I have touched it. I bought wine with it; and it wasn't my money."

His remorse was so apparent that Chester was forced to smile.

"Why, that's all right," he said. "You are going to pay him back. Now come with us."

Again Ivan was silent for several moments.

"That's right," he said at last. "I'm going to pay him back." He rose to his feet. "Come, I shall go with you," and they all passed out into the night.

Clair W. Hayes

CHAPTER XIX

INTO SERBIA

Two days later and we find our friends once more in the air and sailing swiftly toward the rising sun.

"Seems to me we should be along about there some place," declared Hal, taking his eyes from the distance ahead for a brief moment.

"Unless you have not gauged your course accurately," replied Chester.

"I'm sure I have made no mistake," said Hal.

"Then we should be about there."

"About where, that's what I want to know," put in Anthony Stubbs, from his place in the rear of the large army plane, the same in which the four friends had made their escape from the Austrians not so many days before. "Where are we headed for, anyway?"

"That will be a little surprise for you, Mr. Stubbs," Chester returned.

"I'm getting too old to care much about surprises," declared Stubbs. "In the first place, I have no business in this machine, anyhow. I never was much good when my feet were not on the ground, and I feel pretty sick up here."

"Oh, you'll get used to that, Stubbs," spoke up Colonel Anderson.

"Don't you believe it. I've tried it before and I haven't become used to it yet. No, sir. In the first place, a man has got no business up here. If he were meant to fly, he'd have wings, like a bird. I claim it's tempting Providence to go floating about through space in one of these things."

"Well, you didn't seem to hesitate much when we asked you to come," commented Chester.

"Of course not. Think I want to be left alone in this benighted land, with a couple of million Austrians likely to swoop down on it at any minute? I guess not. The air may not be safe, but it can't be any worse than I would have been if I were left behind to await the arrival of the invader. But where are we going?"

"Belgrade," said Chester briefly.

Anthony Stubbs half started to his feet.

"Great Scott!" he exclaimed, and sank back again. "Out of the frying pan into the fire. Say!" and his voice rose a trifle, "What do we want to go to Belgrade for? What's the use of sticking our heads into a hornet's nest?"

"Look here, Mr. Stubbs," said Hal, again turning in his seat. "Don't you want to go to Belgrade with us? If you don't, I'll go down and let you off here."

He reduced the speed of the craft a trifle.

"No, no. Never mind," said Stubbs hurriedly. "I was just joking. Of course I want to go to Belgrade. They tell me that the Germans are just about to come in. But that won't make any difference, will it? No, indeed. Not to us. I suppose we are going to be there to welcome them. I'll bet they'll be glad to see us."

The others smiled, but they made no reply to this outburst. They had known Stubbs long enough now not to pay much attention to him at times. And this was one of those times.

Stubbs now turned a bit in his seat and spoke to another figure who was close to him.

"How do you like this kind of travel, Ivan?" he asked.

"I belong on the ground," was the brief response.

Ivan's face was a chalky white, but he was sitting tight and saying nothing except when it was absolutely necessary. Just behind him sat Nikol, and the latter seemed to be in a condition similar to Ivan. Nor did he make a sound.

Suddenly, as the aeroplane moved swiftly along, there came a loud explosion. The machine rocked crazily and Hal's prompt action at the wheel was all that saved the occupants from being pitched head-first into space. He righted the craft with an effort.

"What's the matter?" demanded Chester in no little alarm.

"It's all over now," mumbled Stubbs with a groan. "Pray, Ivan."

The big Cossack seemed to have no doubt that it was all over and while he clung to the side of the machine with both hands, he mumbled strange words in his native tongue. Apparently he was following Stubbs' injunction.

"I don't know," replied Hal, answering Chester's question. "Something seems to have gone wrong with the engine. Guess we had better go down."

He tilted the elevating levers and the plane descended gradually and swiftly.

Under Hal's firm hand it settled gently upon the ground and all immediately climbed out. Stubbs drew a great breath of relief.

"I never expected to reach here alive," he declared.

Ivan and Nikol also were plainly relieved. They said nothing, but the expression upon both their faces spoke plainer than words.

Hal bent over the engine. As he straightened up, Chester asked:

"Anything serious?"

"Believe I can fix it within an hour," replied Hal. "I'll have a try at it, anyhow."

"Need any assistance?" asked Colonel Anderson.

Hal shook his head.

"Nothing you can do, I guess," he replied.

"Then I am going to take a little prowl into these woods here," said the colonel, indicating a small clump of trees that stood perhaps a quarter of a mile to the east.

"I'll go along," said Chester. "I feel like stretching my legs a bit."

The two walked away together. Ivan and Nikol remained behind and watched Hal tinker with the engine.

Chester and the colonel prowled about among the trees for the better part of half an hour and then turned to make their way back to the machine. As they walked along, Chester suddenly caught Colonel Anderson by the arm, stopping him in his stride.

"Sh-h-h," muttered the lad and listened intently.

"What's the matter?" demanded Colonel Anderson, in a low voice.

"Thought I heard voices," replied Chester. "Listen."

Both became silent; and directly they caught the sound of a low voice off to the right. Then there came a second and a third voice.

"Don't see what they can be doing here, whoever they are," declared Chester in a whisper. "We'll see if we can get a look at them."

He led the way softly in the direction from which the voices had come. The voices became louder; and directly, parting two large bushes, Chester made out the forms of three figures not ten yards away.

He turned quickly to Colonel Anderson and laid a finger to his lips. The colonel approached cautiously.

From the spot where the two stood it was possible to see the three men in front of them without danger of being seen themselves, for they were screened from sight by the large bushes. One of the men was attired in what Chester took to be a Serbian uniform, but the others were in civilian attire.

"We'll do a little eavesdropping," whispered Chester.

Colonel Anderson nodded and they became silent.

"So you say that everything is ready for Bulgaria's entrance into the war?" spoke the man with the uniform.

"Yes," replied one of the others, a man of perhaps forty years of age, with a long flowing beard.

"And she will strike when?"

"The moment Belgrade has fallen before the Germans," replied the third man, who, the watchers saw now, was little more than a boy, smooth of face and bright of eye.

"And they will strike where?"

"At the Anglo-French force being rushed from Saloniki to the aid of the Serbians."

"Why wasn't I kept posted on all this? How was I expected to do my part here, being left in ignorance of diplomatic affairs?"

"I don't know anything about that. All I know is that we were ordered here to learn what success you have had in undermining the Serbian officials. Also to get your views upon which way the Serbians will retreat."

"Well, I can tell you that in a few words. I have had very little success with the Serbians. They are loyal to their cause and seem determined to fight to the last ditch. But I did get close enough to one man—a member of the general staff—to learn that in the event of reverses to Serbian arms, the Serbian army will retreat into Greece."

"So? I had deemed it most likely they would fall back and join the Montenegrins."

"Such is not the plan of the general staff. Their reasons I cannot tell you; but at a guess I should say it is because they hope that, by a juncture with the Anglo-French forces, they may hope to show an effective front until Italy can throw an army to their support, or possibly until the long expected Russian offensive materializes."

"Then we shall have to bring some pressure to bear upon Greece," said the younger man. "We cannot permit that. Bulgaria must get in the game sooner and thus foil such a plan."

"Well, you probably know best," said the officer, "but remember one thing. To all intents and purposes, Bulgaria is still neutral. Announcement that she has decided to cast her lot with the Central Powers, if premature, undoubtedly would spoil many plans. Particularly, if it came to the ears of the Anglo-French commander at Saloniki."

"Exactly," replied the young man. "Our plans now are to permit the Allies to advance a considerable distance toward Belgrade, and then to have Bulgaria declare war at the psychological moment."

"A good plan, that," returned the officer. "But I must get back now. My absence will be noticed and I do not care to arouse suspicion."

The men moved off.

Chester and Colonel Anderson gazed at each other.

"Rather neat little play," said Colonel Anderson.

"Rather," repeated Chester dryly.

"And to think," continued Colonel Anderson, "how leniently Bulgaria has been treated by the Allies. Well, her day of reckoning will come."

"We'll have to get word of this to the Serbian commander in Belgrade," said Chester.

"So we will," said the colonel. "And also to the commander of the Anglo-French forces in Saloniki."

"Let's get back then and see if Hal has the machine fixed so she'll fly."

They retraced their footsteps; and even as they arrived, Hal arose from his position above the aeroplane.

"She'll go now all right," he said. "All aboard!"

Stubbs, Nikol and Ivan hesitated and Stubbs protested. Chester drew Hal aside for a moment and told him what he and the colonel had learned. Hal wasted no further time.

"In here with all of you," he commanded gruffly. "We're going right now."

Clair W. Hayes

The others hesitated no longer, and a few moments later the big machine was flying swiftly toward the Serbian capital.

CHAPTER XX

THE END OF A TRAITOR

It was two years after the outbreak of the great war that the Austro-German armies were hurled forward in a great and final effort to crush Serbia. Since the early days of the struggle, heavy battles had been fought upon the Austro-Serbian frontier, with success first to one side and then to the other.

Belgrade, the Serbian capital, had been bombarded time after time by the great Austrian guns and once the city had been occupied by the foe. Later, however, the Serbians had driven out the invader and reoccupied the capital. And now, the Austrian army, reinforced by a hundred thousand Germans, bringing the total number of troops to half a million, was again knocking at the gates of Belgrade; and the Serbians, realizing the utter hopelessness of their cause unless aid arrived from the Anglo-French troops at Saloniki, were preparing to flee.

This was the situation when the aeroplane bearing Hal, Chester and their friends descended just outside the city.

Hardly had they alighted when they were taken in charge by a squad of Serbian troops. Colonel Anderson, acting as

Clair W. Hayes

spokesman for the party, explained their presence in a few well-chosen words and asked to be taken to the commanding officer. There was considerable red tape to go through before the friends finally were ushered into the presence of the Serbian commander, and that worthy immediately informed them he had but a few moments to give them.

Colonel Anderson, therefore, came to the point at once. He told him of the conversation he and Chester had overheard a short time before.

"And you say one of the men wore a Serbian uniform?" asked the general.

"Yes, sir."

"You don't know who he is—you didn't hear his name mentioned?"

"No, sir; but I would know him again if I saw him."

"Good. You shall have the chance. Now, how far from the city do you say this conversation took place?"

"Must have been all of ten miles, sir."

"Then the men have hardly returned to the city yet. And you say you did not hear the name of the member of the general staff, the first traitor, or spy mentioned as having divulged information?"

"No, sir."

"Very well. Now I will leave all of you here for an hour or so. I have some matters to attend to. When I come back we'll see if you can identify the man you speak of."

The general bowed to them and took his departure, leaving them alone in his quarters.

From without a heavy cannonading could be heard.

"I guess the last advance has begun," said Chester slowly.

"You probably are right," agreed Hal. "And I feel sorry for these Serbians. If the British and French could only get here in time."

"Well, I don't see why they don't," declared Chester. "England has promised more than once since the war began that she would not permit Serbia to be crushed. Seems to me she should have taken some decisive action before now."

"You forget," said Colonel Anderson, "that England has her hands full in other parts of the great war theater—France, Belgium, the Dardanelles, Egypt, India and Africa."

"That's the trouble," said Hal. "England has too many irons in the fire. That's where the Germans and Austrians have the edge, as we say in the United States. Their armies are not scattered all over the world."

"That's true enough," replied Colonel Anderson, "and it is, without doubt, the reason the Central Powers have not been crushed long ago."

Ivan now took a hand in the conversation.

"These wonderful tales you told me of my brother Alexis," he began.

"Well, what of them?" asked Hal.

"Why," said Ivan. "When I came with you I thought I should see some fighting. All I have done is fly through the air, like a bird, and hear a thousand miles of talk. I want to see some fighting, like Alexis saw."

"You probably will see it soon enough," returned Chester quietly. "Even now you can hear the booming of the great guns without. The Austro-Germans are moving on Belgrade and it will only be hours before the Serbian retreat begins."

The conversation continued along various lines until the return of the Serbian commander, General Save.

"If you will come with me," he said to Colonel Anderson, "I will see if you can identify the traitor. Which of your friends here was with you?"

Colonel Anderson nodded toward Chester.

"Then he shall come, too. The others may remain here until we return."

Hal, Ivan and Nikol were undeniably disappointed at this turn of affairs. Not so Stubbs.

"This comes nearer being what I call comfort than anything I have enjoyed since coming across to Europe," he said, settling himself in the commander's easy chair and drawing exhilarating puffs from his pipe. "I don't care how long we stay here."

"Mr. Stubbs," said Hal, "I am afraid you are lazy."

"Mr. Paine," said Stubbs, "I know I'm lazy."

Leaving the general's quarters, Colonel Anderson and

Chester accompanied the Serbian commander toward the front.

"The enemy has begun his advance," General Save explained, as they walked along. "He is attacking in force all along the line. We are resisting as well as we may. That is why every available man has been sent forward. We will find the traitor there some place."

"And do you have any hope of holding back the enemy, sir?" Chester asked.

"None," returned the general quietly. "We will resist to the last, but even now preparations are being made for evacuating the capital. With the coming of darkness, the retreat will begin. We shall fall back to Nish, which, I trust, we shall be able to hold until Anglo-French assistance arrives."

"I hope so, sir," declared Chester.

"And as soon as you have picked out this traitor for me," said General Save, "I will ask you to undertake a mission for me."

"We shall be glad to be of service, sir," replied Colonel Anderson. "And the nature of the mission?"

"Why," said the commander. "I have information to the effect that the Anglo-French troops are already on the way from Saloniki. They may not know of the real seriousness of our position. Communication has been hampered for the last few days. I will send word to them by you."

"Very well, sir," said Colonel Anderson. "We shall be glad to go."

"Now keep your eyes open," said General Save, as they came

for the first time among the Serbian troops, the men farthest from the front, men being held in reserve.

Among the regiments the three passed slowly, scanning the face of every officer; and they came upon their man sooner than they could reasonably have hoped.

Chester suddenly touched General Save on the arm.

"Look! There he is!" the lad said in a low voice.

The general glanced in the direction indicated. Perhaps twenty yards to the left, engaged in conversation with an officer who wore colonel's stripes, and a man whom General Save immediately recognized as one of the general staff, stood the person the lads had seen in the woods a few hours earlier. "Are you sure that is he?" demanded the Serbian commander.

Chester nodded his head vigorously.

"Certain, sir," Colonel Anderson agreed.

"Very good. Then come with me."

The general approached the group of officers, who stood respectfully at attention when they perceived his approach.

"Captain Dellse!" said the General.

"Sir," replied the officer, stepping toward the Serbian commander.

The older officer looked squarely into the man's eyes for several moments without saying a word. The traitor tried his best to return the general's steady gaze and for a moment he succeeded. Then his eyes wavered slightly.

General Save extended his right hand.

"Your sword, sir!" he commanded.

The other staggered back and his face turned a ghastly white.

"Wha—what, sir?" he stammered.

"Your sword," repeated the general calmly, his hand still extended.

With a visible effort the other pulled himself together.

"I do not understand you, sir," he said, with a subdued air of insolence, glancing quickly about at the others who now surrounded him.

General Save lost all patience now. He took a step forward.

"Give me your sword, you traitor!" he commanded angrily. "You are under arrest. You shall be shot in ten minutes."

The face of the accused officer turned livid. There was no pretending to misunderstand now.

Quickly he glanced about him. Chester and Colonel Anderson, in their civilian clothes, stood each with a hand in his right coat pocket, and in the hand of each rested a little automatic.

An ever increasing group of Serbian officers also surrounded him. The man with whom the traitor had been engaged in conversation moved gradually toward the rear of the circle. General Save caught sight of him out of the corner of his eye.

"Colonel Breyold!" he commanded.

The other halted.

"Come here, sir," commanded the general.

Glancing furtively about him, the other obeyed. The Serbian commander turned to another of his officers.

"Relieve Colonel Breyold of his sword," he commanded.

Without waiting to see that his command was carried out, he stepped close to Dellse. The other gave way before him and with a sudden movement produced a revolver.

Before those nearby could interfere, he had raised the weapon and pulled the trigger. There was a sharp report, a flash of fire, and when the smoke had cleared away, Dellse and General Save were locked in each other's embrace, struggling furiously.

With loud cries other Serbian officers jumped forward and separated the combatants. Dellse's weapon was wrested from his grasp and in a moment he was powerless.

"Are you hurt, sir?" asked one of the officers anxiously of the general.

"No," was the reply.

With a gesture of his arm, he indicated the two traitors. "Take them out and shoot them immediately!" he ordered.

CHAPTER XXI

ACROSS MACEDONIA

"No," said Hal, "I am afraid to take a chance with our old airplane. It hasn't been gone over thoroughly yet. If General Save is anxious for us to go at once, Chester, you and Colonel Anderson go on ahead. I'll look our machine over and follow you."

"Well, whatever you say," said Chester. "The general is anxious that we start at once and perhaps the way you suggest will do as well as another."

"I'm going with the first party," declared Ivan at this juncture. "I'm tired of sitting about doing nothing. I want to be on the move. If something doesn't happen pretty soon, I'm going back to the Albanian Mountains."

"I'll be glad to have you go with me," said Chester. "Hal, you can bring Stubbs and Nikol with you."

Hal nodded.

"All right. Then you had better see the general about a craft of some kind."

Chester hastened away, but was back a few moments later with the announcement that General Save would have a plane ready for them within the hour.

Hal and Chester then examined a map of the country carefully and laid out a course. It was agreed that Hal should follow the same course, for, as Chester said, there was little likelihood of anything going wrong, but coming along the same route the second craft would always have a chance of rendering aid should it be needed. The lads agreed to meet at Saloniki the following day.

It was nearly dark when the machine carrying Chester, Colonel Anderson and Ivan soared in the air and headed south over Macedonia—once the kingdom of Philip and Alexander the Great. Stubbs, Nikol and Hal watched their friends disappear in the distance with some misgiving, which was given expression by Stubbs.

"I hope they get there safely," he muttered, "but I have my doubts."

"See here, Mr. Stubbs," said Hal. "You've gone through a lot, but you are still here, aren't you?"

"I am," said Stubbs calmly, "but I wish I were some place else."

"Well, give me an hour or two to look over our machine and you will soon be some place else," said Hal.

"And the chances are I'd rather be some place than where I am likely to be if I keep monkeying around in the air," replied the little man.

Hal raised both hands in a gesture of hopelessness.

"There's no use talking to you," he said. "I'll leave you both here while I overhaul the plane."

He took himself off.

Chester, Colonel Anderson and Ivan sailed swiftly through the air. Darkness fell, but it was a bright night and Chester, at the wheel, could see without difficulty. The passengers were quite comfortable in spite of the cold.

"Aren't you getting a bit too low?" asked Colonel Anderson after a couple of hours flying in the darkness.

"Thousand feet," said Chester after a glance at the indicator.

"Doesn't seem like it to me," said the colonel. "Think I can see the ground below."

"You shouldn't at this altitude," said Chester.

"I know it. Guess I was mistaken."

Half an hour later the colonel spoke again. "Have you come down any, Chester?"

"No; why?"

"I'm sure I can see the ground below," returned the colonel.

Chester glanced over the side of the plane.

"By Jove! So can I," he exclaimed. He glanced at the indicator again. It still read a trifle over a thousand feet. "Something wrong some place," he said to himself.

He tilted the elevating lever, but the plane did not answer by a sudden rush upward. Chester gave a long whistle.

"What's the matter?' demanded Colonel Anderson.

"I don't know," returned Chester. "We're going down gradu-ally, I know that, but the indicator still reads a thousand feet and I can't move the plane any higher."

"And you don't know what is wrong?"

"Haven't the slightest idea. I'm no airship expert."

"Then you shouldn't try to run one," declared Ivan.

"Now don't get worried, Ivan," said Chester with a laugh. "We'll get down again all right."

"We'll probably get down," said Ivan, "but the thing that worries me is whether it will be all right or not. I want to die with my feet on the ground and not be dashed against the earth head first."

"I'm sure there is no danger," said Chester. "We're just sinking gently."

He cut off the engine and allowed the craft to volplane to earth more abruptly. It came to rest on the ground as lightly as a bird.

"Well, what will we do now?" demanded Ivan.

"You have as much idea as I have," returned Chester. "I can't fix this thing here in the darkness; in fact, I don't know whether I can fix it at all. We'll either have to walk or stay here until I can have a look at this craft in daylight—and maybe that won't do any good."

"I vote we walk," said Colonel Anderson. "There must be houses along here some place. Maybe we can commandeer three horses, or an automobile or something."

"Most likely what we'll commandeer will be trouble," grumbled Ivan.

"Now what are you kicking about?" demanded Chester. "You have been hunting trouble ever since I have known you. Maybe you'll be satisfied this time."

"Do you think so?" demanded Ivan eagerly.

"No, I don't," returned Chester. "If I did I'd sit right here. I don't want to run into any trouble now if I can help it. We've got business on hand, remember that. And we've got to hurry. Colonel Anderson, I guess your suggestion is a good one. We'll walk on a ways."

They set out without a word. Striking across what appeared in the darkness a large field, they eventually came to a road. They walked south along this.

Half an hour later, in the darkness, there loomed up a house ahead of them. A faint light glowed in the window.

"Told you there must be a house along here some place," said Colonel Anderson.

Chester produced his watch and succeeded in reading the face after some trouble.

"Lacks five minutes to midnight," he said. "Rather a late hour to be making a call."

"Necessity knows no law," responded Colonel Anderson.

"We won't bother them much, if they can furnish us with some means of transportation."

"Hope they will be friendly," said Chester.

"No reason why they shouldn't be. I suppose we are still in Serbia."

"Well, I don't know whether we are or not. That's what worries me," said Chester.

"Why, where do you think we are?"

"I don't know. Might be Serbia, might be Greece, might be Bulgaria, or Turkey or any old place. If the elevating apparatus on our plane was out of whack, the steering apparatus may have been, too. Also I have mislaid my compass. I won't know north from south until morning."

"Hm-m-m," muttered the colonel. "Well, shall we try this house?"

"May as well, I guess," said Chester.

He led the way to the front door and rapped sharply with his knuckles.

There was a sound of some one stirring within, but no face appeared at the door in response to the lad's knock. He rapped sharply again. This time there was not a sound from within.

Chester walked a little ways from the house and glanced at the window through which a light had been visible a few moments before. It was perfectly dark now. Apparently the light had been extinguished the moment he had rapped on the door. All was dark within.

Chester moved toward the house again, thinking to rap on the door once more. As he did so, there came the sound of a shot and Chester felt something whistle by his ear.

"Wow!" he cried, and dashed toward the door where Colonel Anderson and Ivan stood.

"Hit?" cried Colonel Anderson, as the lad dashed up.

"No," replied Chester. "But that bullet didn't miss me much. What'll we do now?"

"I don't really know. We don't know where we are. Why not spend the night here?"

"For one reason," said Chester grimly, "because they won't let us in."

"Oh, we can fix that. Break in the door."

"And get shot for our pains."

"No, I don't think so. My impression is that there is no more than a single occupant of the house. That's the reason he was frightened when we knocked. We'll just go in where it's warm and pay no further attention to him."

"Well, whatever you say," said Chester. "Stand back there, till I blow the lock off that door." He drew his revolver.

"Hold on," said Ivan. "I'll open it"

He stepped back a pace, then rushed forward. His huge shoulder came into contact with the hard wood and there was

Clair W. Hayes

a crash as the door gave way beneath his weight.

Ivan went in unhesitatingly and the others followed him.

Inside Chester struck a match.

"Look out!" cried Colonel Anderson. "Want to get us all shot?"

"We've got to see where we are going," said Chester.

The glare of a match showed them a room to the right of the hall. Chester led the way in, still holding the match above his head. On the stand in the center of the room was a big lamp. Chester lighted it.

"Evidently," he said, "this is the same light we saw when we came up."

The three now pulled themselves close to a fire that glowed softly in an open fireplace and made themselves comfortable.

"We might as well get a little sleep," said Chester. "Anderson, you take first watch. Call me in two hours. I'm going to sleep here."

He closed his eyes, then opened them suddenly again. He had heard a slight noise.

Stepping quickly across to a table at the far end of the room, he stooped down and, thrusting his revolver under the table, called:

"Come out!"

There was a faint rustling and a sound as of some one crying.

Then a figure, rumpled and fearful, came from beneath the table; and Chester cried:

"A girl!"

Clair W. Hayes

CHAPTER XXII

ATTACKED

Chester's exclamation was wrung from him in English. At the sound of his words the girl looked at him quickly and clasping her hands imploringly, cried out:

"Don't kill me!"

Her words were also in English and she spoke without the slightest accent. Chester and Colonel Anderson looked at her dumfounded.

"Are you English?" demanded Chester, taking a step toward her.

The girl staggered back.

"Keep away, please," she said.

"Are you English?" repeated Chester.

The girl recovered herself with an effort and forced herself to answer the lad's question calmly.

"No," she said, "I am an American."

"An American!" exclaimed Chester. "You are an American?"

"Yes," cried the girl, "and you will harm me at your peril. The United States—"

"Uncle Sam is a long ways off," said Chester quietly. "But I guess he can take care of you. I, too am an American."

"You!" exclaimed the girl eagerly, taking a step forward. Then, after a quick glance at his clothes, she shrank back.

Chester smiled.

"Don't judge me by these garments," he said. "I assure you I am an American, and my friend here," he indicated Colonel Anderson, "is a British officer. My other friend," pointing to Ivan, "is a Russian. So you see, you are among friends."

"Are you telling me the truth?" asked the girl fearfully, eying Chester searchingly.

"It is a habit I have," replied Chester quietly. "Yes, I am an American and if you have a mind to question me about anything American you will find that I am telling you the truth."

"What is your name?" asked the girl.

"Chester Crawford."

"Chester Crawford!"

Again the girl looked at him searchingly.

At last she asked: "And do you know another young American named Hal Paine?"

"Hal!" exclaimed Chester, startled at hearing his friend's name from this girl whom he had, to his knowledge, never seen before. "Of course. He is my chum. But he has never told me he knew a girl answering your description."

"Oh, I don't know him," replied the girl. "But I have heard of you both from a friend—a girl friend; and if you can tell me her name, I will be sure that you are Chester Crawford."

"How can I tell you?" asked Chester. "I know several girls. Was it Mary—"

"This girl," was the reply, "you met in Belgium. If you are truly Chester Crawford you will know who I mean."

"Do you mean Miss Johnson—Edna Johnson?" inquired Chester.

A happy smile lighted up the girl's face.

"I do! I do!" she exclaimed. "It was Edna Johnson. She wrote me a letter, telling me how she met two young American boys in Belgium and giving me their names. I have heard from her often and each time she has mentioned your names. She wonders what has become of you."

"Well," said Chester with a smile. "I'm here and Hal is some place between here and Belgrade, I expect. Now will you tell me who you are?"

"I am Helen Ellison of St. Louis," replied the girl, extending her hand.

Chester took the hand and turned to the others.

"Allow me to present my friends to you," he said quietly.

"Colonel Anderson, of His British Majesty's service."

Colonel Anderson bowed.

"And Ivan Vergoff,"—this in French. "Ivan, Mademoiselle Ellison."

The big Cossack also bowed and acknowledged the introduction.

The girl smiled at both of them, and Chester was glad to learn that she understood French.

"And now," he said, "if you will tell me exactly where we are, I shall be greatly obliged."

The girl looked at him in surprise.

"You don't know where you are?" she asked.

Chester shook his head.

"You are now," said Helen, "just across the Serbian border from Bulgaria. This house is the home of a friend of mine, Miss Thatcher, a Red Cross nurse. I met her in Belgrade where she was wounded. When it became evident that the Austrians were about to occupy the city, we came to the home of her friend here, a Serbian woman. That was before there was any talk of Bulgaria joining Germany. But now that war has been declared—"

"War declared!" exclaimed Chester.

"Why, I think so. Maybe there has been no declaration of war, but anyhow the Serbians and Bulgarians have been fighting across the frontier. That's why I was so afraid when you knocked at the door to-night."

"And it was you who shot at me?" asked Chester.

"Yes," replied the girl. "And, oh, I am so sorry. If—"

"Never mind," said Chester soothingly. "You didn't hit me."

"I know I didn't, but I—"

"There, there, now," said Chester. "And where is your friend now?"

"She went away this morning and she hasn't come back yet."

"Do you know where she went?"

"Yes; to the home of a peasant about six miles from here. His wife is sick and Miss Thatcher has been attending them since she has been well enough to do so."

"And you were left here all along?" said Chester.

"Yes, but I wasn't afraid until this afternoon, when half a dozen Bulgarians crossed the frontier and tried to get in the house."

"The did?" exclaimed Chester angrily. "I wish we had been here."

"So do I," said Helen. "They knocked on the door, but I wouldn't let them in. Then they threatened to break the door down, but an officer came up at that moment and ordered them away. They went sulkily and one of them called back that they would return. That's why I was afraid when you knocked a little while ago."

"And no wonder," replied Chester. "It must have been a terrible day for you."

"It has indeed," said the girl weakly.

Chester sprang toward her quickly and took her gently by the arms, just as it seemed she would fall over in a faint. He seated her in a chair, and poured her a glass of water from a pitcher on a nearby table.

After drinking the water the girl appeared refreshed.

"So foolish of me to get weak like that," she said, smiling.

"It's no wonder," returned Chester. "It's just the reaction. You'll be all right in a minute or two."

The lad was a good prophet; and five minutes later Helen was talking and laughing vivaciously. All four were having a good time, when Chester's ears caught a faint sound from without.

The lad paused as he was about to say something in reply to one of Helen's questions and listened intently.

"What's the matter?" asked Helen.

"Oh, nothing," said Chester, and continued his remarks.

A few moments later, however, he arose, and asking to be excused for a moment, stepped toward the door which Ivan had broken to permit their entrance; just beyond he caught sight of a dark shadow.

"As I thought," he muttered. "They have come back."

He returned to the door of the parlor and summoned the big Cossack.

"Oh, Ivan," he called. "Come out here a minute."

The Cossack came up to him and Chester led him toward the door.

"What can you see out there?" he asked.

Ivan poked his head out and looked around.

"Ho!" he exclaimed suddenly and leaped out.

A moment later Chester heard the sound of a brief struggle and then Ivan reappeared dragging a man after him.

"I've got him," said the giant, laughing loudly.

The laughter attracted the attention of Helen and Colonel Anderson, who came from the parlor to learn the cause of it.

Helen gave a cry of fear as her eyes fell upon Ivan's prisoner.

"Who is he?" she exclaimed.

"Oh, just some fellow who was spooking around outside," replied Chester.

But Helen was not to be fooled thus easily.

"It is one of the Bulgarians who were here this afternoon,' she cried, and addressed the man in his own tongue. Then she turned to the others. "He says the others are coming," she cried. "He came on ahead of them."

"Oh, is that so?" said Chester quietly. "Well, they'll have a different reception this time."

He told the others what the girl had learned.

Colonel Anderson received the news quietly.

"We'll be ready for them," he said.

But Ivan was not so calm when he heard what Helen had told Chester.

"So there is going to be a fight at last, eh?" he cried in a loud voice. "What are a dozen or so of these Bulgarians? I know them of old. Cowards and traitors all. I have had an experience with more than one of them. We are good for a dozen or two of them, if we can keep them in front of us. Oh, yes, the Bulgarians are great fighters—from behind."

"Is there any way we can fix up that door?" asked Chester.

Colonel Anderson shook his head.

"I am afraid not. Ivan has shattered it beyond repair."

"Then it shall be my post to guard," cried Ivan. "No Bulgarian shall come through there."

"There are not many other places they can come through," said Helen. "Only two windows and a second door, in the rear of the house. I shall guard one of the windows myself."

"You are not afraid?" asked Chester.

"Not now, that I have friends with me."

Clair W. Hayes

"All right. Colonel Anderson, I'll take this other window here, near Miss Ellison. You shall guard the back door."

"The first thing to do is tie this fellow up," said Anderson, indicating the Bulgarian.

Ivan stepped forward, and taking a piece of rope that Helen gave him, tied the man up tightly.

"Now," said Chester, "to your posts. We don't want to be caught unguarded."

All took the places assigned them and examined their weapons. An hour passed. Then Chester, peering through the window, exclaimed:

"Here they come!"

CHAPTER XXIII

THE FIGHT IN THE HOUSE

"I'm ready for them!" shouted Ivan, from his position behind the broken door.

He stood well back in the darkness, out of sight from beyond the house.

All was quiet and dark within, for with the appearance of the first of the enemy Chester had extinguished the light. The figures of the approaching Bulgarians were plainly visible to Chester and Helen through the windows. Ivan and Colonel Anderson, of course, could not see them, although they would have been visible to the former had he a mind to take a chance and expose himself to their view.

As the men approached, Chester counted them. Then he announced:

"Thirteen, I make them."

"My count, too," agreed Helen from her window.

There was not a tremor in her voice now and she seemed totally unlike the frightened girl Chester had first seen. She

　　　　　Clair W. Hayes

held her revolver steadily in her right hand, a pile of ammunition heaped up in the window sill before her.

The men came on briskly, absolutely unaware of the rude welcome that awaited them.

"Let them get close enough so we can't miss, then I'll hold a parley with them," said Chester.

When the men were less than fifty yards from the house, Chester raised his voice and called out sternly in Russian:

"Halt there!"

The Bulgarians halted in their tracks and gazed about in surprise. To the best of their knowledge there could be no one in the house but the girl, and this sudden hail in a male voice made them pause.

"What do you want here?" demanded Chester from his shelter.

There was a hurried consultation among the enemy; then one man called:

"We want to get in."

"You can't get in," returned Chester calmly.

There was a roar of laughter from without.

"Did you hear that?" said one. "He says we can't get in." The man called to Chester: "And who is going to stop us?"

"You'll find there are enough of us here for that purpose," replied the lad evenly. "I warn you we'll shoot the next step forward you take."

Again those without held a consultation and Chester could barely make out the trend of the conversation.

"Perhaps they are too many for us," said one.

"Nonsense," was the reply of another. "He's simply trying to frighten us away. We'll rush the two windows and the doors at the same time. Some of us will get in."

"All right. Whatever you say—"

"Come on then."

The men split up suddenly into four separate bodies and rushed forward.

"Let 'em have it," said Chester quietly.

His revolver spoke at the same moment as did that of Helen and two men stumbled as they ran. One recovered himself instantly and came on, but the other pitched forward to the ground.

Colonel Anderson, at the rear door, remained at his post. There was nothing he could do until the enemy attempted to force the door.

Ivan, however, stepped quickly from his place of conceal-ment and standing erect in the doorway fired point blank at the four men who came dashing toward him. One threw up his hands with a cry and a second muttered a fierce imprecation. Ivan emptied his revolver and then dashed back to safety even as a fusillade was fired at him. The Cossack was untouched. He smiled grimly to himself.

"Not so bad," he muttered.

He reloaded in haste and again stepped into the open. The men before his post, the three who remained upon their feet, were directly in front of the door and all fired simultaneously as Ivan showed himself. The big Cossack felt a stinging sensation in his left arm, but he did not pause to investigate the wound.

Again he raised his weapon quickly and fired its contents toward his foes. But Ivan's aim was poor—or he had fired without aiming—for not a bullet went home. Again Ivan dodged back just in time.

The men who had advanced toward the two windows had been driven off by Helen and Chester. Two of their number lay on the ground and two of the others were nursing wounded arms. Out of revolver-shot they stopped and discussed the situation.

In the rear, the men who had attacked there were even now knocking at the door with their revolver butts. Chester heard Colonel Anderson's voice:

"Get away from there, or I shall fire through the door."

There came a loud report and Chester believed for a moment the colonel had been as good as his word. But he was soon undeceived.

"They've blown the lock off the door," cried the colonel. "Guess they'll try to rush me now."

"You guard both these windows for a moment," said Chester. "I'll lend Anderson a hand."

He hurried back and arrived just in time to see the door swing inward. Colonel Anderson, across the room from the door, stood in the shadow, waiting for the first of the enemy to show himself.

The door swung back violently and the men appeared in the opening in a body. Chester and Colonel Anderson fired almost together. Came hoarse cries from the attackers and a moment later the doorway was cleared. Immediately Chester and the colonel hurled their weight against it, closing it again.

"Safe for a minute," said Chester.

He hastened back to where he had left Helen and arrived just in time to see the girl fire her revolver at a figure that dashed toward the house. The man did not falter. Apparently the girl's aim had been bad. The man dashed to the very side of the house and took his stand directly under the window.

Chester poked his head out to see if he could pick the man off and as he did so his cap leaped from his head. The lad heard something whiz by. He withdrew his head quickly.

"Just missed me," he said quietly.

Now three forms came dashing toward the house, running in a zig-zag course.

"See if you can get one of them," cried Chester to the girl.

He took deliberate aim himself and fired. One man dropped.

Helen also fired—twice, but the other two men came on and joined the first arrival under the edge of the window.

Clair W. Hayes

"Great Scott! This won't do," said Chester. "We can't have those fellows under there. We'll have to get them out some way."

At that moment Colonel Anderson's voice rang out:

"Here they come again."

Chester dashed back. Again the door swung inward and two faces appeared, revolvers leveled before them. They fired even as they came in sight and Colonel Anderson tumbled over with a sharp cry.

"They got me," he said in a faint voice.

"And I got one of them!" shouted Chester as one of the Bulgarians hit the floor with a thud.

The other withdrew his head before Chester could fire again.

Chester raised his voice and called to Helen:

"How are you making it?"

"All right," the girl called back. "Haven't seen any one since you left."

"Can you hold both windows?" demanded Chester.

"I think so. Why?"

"Anderson has been hit. I'll have to stand guard here. Pass the word to Ivan, will you? Tell him of the men under the window. He may be able to help you out."

The girl did as Chester ordered.

Helen, standing close to the window, allowed her revolver to rest on the sill. In the darkness, a hand appeared from below and grasped the weapon by the barrel and wrenched it from her grasp before she could pull the trigger.

Helen screamed.

"What's the matter?" cried Chester anxiously.

"I've lost my gun," said the girl. "And here they come in the window!"

"I'm coming!" cried Chester, and started forward.

But another figure beat him. It was the giant form of Ivan.

"You stand here," he said sternly. "Guard both doors and the windows as you value your lives. I'll attend to the others."

He moved toward the shattered door without another word.

"Where are you going?" demanded Chester anxiously.

Ivan disappeared without making reply.

At that moment one of the men who had succeeded in forcing the rear door came dashing through the house. He held his revolver ready, but he didn't see Chester quickly enough. Chester raised his own weapon and took a snapshot. The man threw up both arms and staggered back. Immediately Chester leaped forward and possessed himself of the other's revolver, which he passed to Helen.

A second form appeared in the doorway and fired at Chester. But the lad had perceived his opponent just in time to leap back and the bullet went wild. Bringing his own revolver forward in deliberate aim, Chester dropped the other with a single shot.

"Look!" cried Helen from the window at this moment.

Chester did so and saw the remainder of the Bulgarians coming toward the house at a dead run. He put his revolver out the window and fired twice. Helen did the same.

But both had fired too quickly and all the bullets went wide. The men pulled up under the window, out of the range of fire from within, safely enough, and Chester and Helen could hear them talking.

"We'll wait here," said one. "Somebody'll show his head pretty quick and when he does, we'll get him."

Chester motioned to Helen to move back from the window.

"What are you going to do?" she asked in some anxiety.

"Have you any hot water?" asked Chester suddenly.

"Why, yes," cried the girl and clapped her hands, "There is a kettle on the stove."

"You remain here while I get it," said Chester briefly.

He dashed into the kitchen and was back in a moment with the large kettle of hot water in both hands. He motioned the girl away from the window.

The lad lifted the kettle to the sill with an effort, and then gauging the position of the enemy by the sound of the voices without, he tilted it over.

Came furious cries of pain from without as the boiling water found its mark. Then there came a different sort of cry. Chester looked out quickly.

From the front door dashed Ivan and bore down upon the foe.

Clair W. Hayes

CHAPTER XXIV

IVAN SHOWS HIS METAL

Chester had poured the boiling water upon the foe at the psychological moment indeed—for Ivan had been ready to dash forward at that exact minute and Chester had diverted the attention of the Bulgarians long enough for Ivan to reach them without being discovered.

Had the men not been otherwise engaged when he dashed from his place of concealment, they would doubtless have shot him down before he reached them. But the kettle of hot water had prevented them from bringing their revolvers to bear until too late.

Ivan descended upon them with a wild cry, and at sight of him the Bulgarians gave back. Eight of them there were, but they recoiled as a single man from the great Cossack.

A single shot Ivan fired from his two revolvers and then they were empty. Quickly he reversed both weapons, and holding both by the barrels, he was among the enemy, striking right and left as fast as the eye could see.

Down went a man on the left with a cracked skull. A man on the right caught a glancing blow on the shoulder and also toppled over. Now the remaining six scattered and sought to get a position where they could shoot Ivan down without fear of injuring one of their own number. But Ivan prevented this by keeping close.

He at length seized one man by the neck—dropping the revolver he held in his left hand to do so—and held him before him as a shield.

Then he charged the others.

Ivan's eyes shone with a terrible fire as he darted forward. His hat was off and his long hair streamed in the wind. Holding his human shield as he did with his strong left hand, he raised his revolver aloft in his right, gripping it tightly by the barrel.

The nearest man of the enemy failed to skip aside quickly enough and the revolver crashed down on his head with a thud. That was the last of him. A second, thinking to take advantage of this action, slipped upon the giant from behind and leveled his revolver at Ivan's head. But once more Ivan was too quick for him, and, whirling suddenly, hurled his revolver at the man.

The Cossack's aim was true, and struck squarely in the face with the sharp revolver, the man dropped to the ground. Now, besides the man he still held aloft, there were but three of the enemy left. With a loud cry, they turned and ran.

But Ivan had no mind to be balked of his prey. He still held a weapon, and he made good use of it. The weapon was the man he had been using for a shield. Raising him high above his head with his right arm, he hurled him forward, as a man putting the shot.

Clair W. Hayes

The human catapult sailed through the air and struck two of the enemy as it fell, carrying them to the ground, knocking the breath from the bodies of all three.

Ivan leaped forward quickly. Stooping, he picked up two men, one in each hand, and brought their heads together with an audible crash. Then he hurled one down upon the third man with great force, and stooping, picked up a revolver.

Quickly he dropped to one knee, and leveling the revolver, took careful aim at the remaining man, who was now some distance away and running swiftly.

"Crack!"

A report, a flash of flame in the darkness.

An imprecation from Ivan, a second report and flash of flame, and the man fell sprawling.

Ivan rose calmly. He surveyed the field of action with a critical eye. Then, without a word, he turned on his heel and stalked back to the house. As he came to where Chester and Helen stood, he said quietly:

"Any more of them in here?"

"None," returned Chester. "You finished the lot."

"Good," said the Cossack. "I thought they had me once."

He uttered no further word, but made his way to the parlor, where he sat down as calmly as though nothing had happened.

"You go in there, too," said Chester to Helen. "I'll have a look at Anderson."

But the girl refused to obey this command and accompanied the lad to where the gallant Colonel lay, moaning feebly.

Chester dropped down and raised Colonel Anderson's head to his knee.

"How do you feel, old man?" he asked.

"Rather weak and dizzy," was the Colonel's mumbled response.

"Where did the bullet hit you?"

"Top of the head some place," and Colonel Anderson raised a feeble hand and passed it over his head.

"Quiet now," said Chester. "I'll have you in the other room in a jiffy and we'll have a look at the wound. Will you make a light in the parlor, Miss Ellison?"

The girl hastened away to do as Chester requested and the lad assisted Colonel Anderson to his feet.

"Put your arm around my neck," the lad commanded. "Lean all your weight on me and I'll drag you into the other room. You're too big for me to carry."

Colonel Anderson followed instructions and Chester dragged him to the parlor, where he laid him on a couch. Then he bent over and examined the wound.

"Doesn't amount to much," he said finally, rising. "Will you get me some water and a cloth. Miss Ellison? Also, if by any chance you can find it, a piece of adhesive plaster."

"I can get them all," said the girl. "Miss Thatcher's kit is

Clair W. Hayes

still here."

She hurried away and was back in a few minutes with the necessary things. She lent Chester a hand and bathed the wound on the Colonel's head, while Chester unrolled the adhesive plaster. Then they bound up the wound.

Colonel Anderson then insisted on sitting up. He passed a hand ruefully across his bandaged head and smiled faintly.

"Hurts a little, but not much," he said in answer to Chester's question. "But now, if you'll tell me—"

He paused suddenly and raised a warning hand.

"What's the matter now?" demanded Chester anxiously.

"Thought I heard voices without."

With a bound Ivan left his chair and darted toward the door. He disappeared in the darkness.

"Ivan's fighting blood is up," said Chester. "I guess I'd better go after him. You guard the wounded man here, Miss Ellison."

He hurried after Ivan.

Outside the door he came upon a strange sight—a sight that caused him to cry out in merriment and thankfulness.

In his first gaze he saw four figures and the first he recognized as that of Hal, the next that of Nikol. These two stood quietly gazing at two other figures who were struggling nearby. Chester glanced at the other figures. They were Ivan and Anthony Stubbs and they appeared to be locked in a death grapple.

"Help! Help!" came Stubbs' voice.

Chester moved forward to interfere, for he reasoned that perhaps Ivan, in his lust for battle, had been unable to distinguish between friend and foe. But Hal stayed him with uplifted hand and Chester saw that his chum was laughing quietly. He realized then that Ivan had recognized his opponent.

He lined up with Hal and Nikol and watched the struggle.

Ivan had one huge arm around the little man and seemed to be making strenuous efforts to throw him. Stubbs struggled valiantly, the while sending out wails for help. Chester saw that Ivan was simply playing.

"Stick to him, Mr. Stubbs," cried Chester. "You'll have him down in a minute."

Stubbs twisted and squirmed like an eel. Once he slipped free of Ivan's clutch and started to run. Ivan reached out quickly and grasped him by the left shoulder and drew him back.

Stubbs let out a yell of fear, and as he turned face to face with the Cossack, he struck out and upward with his clenched fist. The blow landed squarely on Ivan's nose and brought a stream of blood.

Ivan let out a roar of rage. Apparently he had not bargained for this. Then he lifted Stubbs high, in the air and tossed him away in the darkness. The little man's yells were loud and long as he flew through the air. He struck the hard earth with a grunt perhaps twenty feet away.

Clair W. Hayes

Slowly he got to his feet and came toward the others, who were now talking to Ivan. In front of them, he stopped.

"Say!" he exclaimed. "What are you fellows trying to do, anyhow? Get me killed off so you won't have to bother with me? Didn't you see that big heathen tossing me around? What?"

Hal turned and eyed the little man suddenly.

"Why, there he is now," he said in a voice of surprise. "We were just talking about you, Mr. Stubbs. Chester was asking about you. I told him you were here a moment ago. Where did you go so suddenly?"

Stubbs glared at them.

"You mean to tell me you didn't see some big giant grab me a minute ago?" he demanded. "You didn't see me fighting for my life?"

"Fighting?" exclaimed Hal. "You fighting, Mr. Stubbs. I didn't think you would attack a man."

"I didn't attack a man," shouted the thoroughly aroused Stubbs. "I didn't attack a man. A man attacked me. No, it wasn't a man, either. It was a giant."

"Is that so, Mr. Stubbs?" asked Chester in well-feigned surprise. "And where were the rest of us all that time?"

"Where—where were you?" echoed Stubbs. "You were right here, that's where you were. You mean to tell me you didn't hear me call for help?"

"You don't say," said Hal. "Why didn't you call aloud,

Mr. Stubbs?"

Stubbs sputtered angrily.

"By George! I did call out loud," he cried.

"And what has happened to the man who attacked you, Mr. Stubbs—the giant you speak of?" inquired Hal civilly.

"Well, he, I—I don't know. He looked suspiciously like Ivan there to me, though why he should jump me, I don't know. Yes, sir, I could have sworn it was Ivan, but I must have been mistaken."

Stubbs glanced around on all sides.

"By George!" he exclaimed at last. "I know I had a fight, but I can't seem to make any one believe it."

"Still sleepy, Mr. Stubbs?" asked Hal.

"Sleepy?" repeated the little man. "Sleepy? What do you mean?"

"Why, that fighting dream just now," said Hal. For a moment Stubbs stared at the lad angrily; then turned on his heel and stalked into the house.

"Come," said Chester, with a laugh, "I'll take you into the house, Hal, and introduce you to a real nice little girl. She's heard of you. She told me so. Come on."

Clair W. Hayes

CHAPTER XXV

BETWEEN TWO FIRES

At the door to the parlor, Chester stopped stock still. The others halted behind him.

"Now what do you think of that?" he demanded.

Inside, Stubbs was standing before Helen Ellison.

"Yes," he was saying, "I am Anthony Stubbs, war correspondent of the *New York Gazette*. I am here on important business. But I have other worries besides my work. I am burdened with the care of two young American boys. I have to look after them and keep them out of trouble. Hal Paine and Chester Crawford. Perhaps you know them?"

The little man paused expectantly.

"I have met Chester Crawford," was the reply. "He was here only a moment ago. I do not know Hal Paine."

"Well, if you know one of them you are just one better off than I am," was Stubbs' rejoinder. "I know them both, too well. Were it not that I am continually giving up my time to getting them out of scrapes, I would be able to give more attention to my own work. You should be glad that you know but one of them."

"But I thought—" began the girl.

Stubbs interrupted her with a wave of his hand.

"Oh, I know what you thought," he said. "I thought so myself once. So have lots of others. But if you knew them as well as I do you'd change your mind."

"Well, what do you think of it?" asked Chester of Hal, in a whisper.

"I think it's about time we went in," returned Hal.

Chester advanced into the room and the others followed. Stubbs turned guiltily.

"Oh, there you are," he said. "I was just telling this young lady here what great friends we all are. Yes, sir. I just remarked that if she were in any kind of danger, to mention it to you and you boys would see that no harm came to her."

"Are you sure that's what you were talking about, Mr. Stubbs?" asked Chester.

"Why, of course. What did you think?"

"Well, I thought perhaps you might have told Miss Ellison of all the trouble we have caused you."

Stubbs started.

"I—I—" he stammered.

"Oh, we heard you, Mr. Stubbs," said Hal.

"Well," said Stubbs with ruffled dignity. "Eavesdroppers never hear any good of themselves." But the little man soon recovered his poise. "I was just joking," he said. "I knew you boys were listening. Ha! Ha!" He eyed Chester. "The young lady here says she has met you," he said. "You young rascal, so this is why you wanted to come on ahead, is it?"

Chester blushed.

"See here, Mr. Stubbs," he began, "I—"

"Ha! Ha!" laughed Stubbs. He approached Chester and gave him a dig in the ribs with his thumb. "So," he exclaimed, and added, "well, I was young myself once."

He had successfully turned the tables on Chester and he was now very much pleased with himself.

Chester decided that the best policy was to ignore the little man's remarks, so he turned the conversation by introducing Hal and Nikol to Helen. Then, when all were on speaking terms, he turned to Hal.

"Tell me how you happened to find us?" he asked.

"It's simple enough," was the reply. "As we were sailing along, I heard shots below. I came down to investigate. The first thing I knew, after coming in sight of this house, I saw a great hulk of a man come rushing out. I drew my revolver and was about to fire when I recognized Ivan. At first I wasn't sure whether Ivan knew us, but when he grabbed Stubbs there and began to play with him, I knew he did. So Nikol and I stood back and watched. Then you came out. That's all I have to tell."

"And so you admit it wasn't a dream," exclaimed Stubbs angrily. "A fine lot of friends you are. How do you know what that untamed heathen might have done to me?"

"Heathen, am I?" exclaimed Ivan, getting to his feet.

"No, no! I didn't mean that," said Stubbs, backing away. "I apologize."

Ivan resumed his seat and Stubbs continued:

"I just want to tell you I don't think much of such treatment. As I have told you before, you rush to each other's aid fast enough, but when I get in a tight place I am left to fight it out by myself."

"And you always come out on top, Mr. Stubbs," declared Chester. "We would deprive you of none of the glory."

"Yes, but some of these times I won't come out on top and then what good will glory do me, huh?"

"Think how proud Mrs. Stubbs—"

"I can tell you right now that Mrs. Stubbs is not looking for glory," shouted Stubbs. "What Mrs. Stubbs wants is me and if I fool around with you much longer I'm mighty likely to disappoint her."

Stubbs stalked across the room and sat down in a corner.

"Tell me," said Hal to Chester, "what was all the shooting about?"

"Oh, it didn't amount to much," returned Chester. "Thirteen Bulgarians attacked us. That's all. Anderson, Miss Ellison

Clair W. Hayes

and I disposed of a couple and Ivan here attended to the rest. They are all dead now, I guess."

"And where is Anderson?" demanded Hal.

"Over there on the sofa," said Chester, pointing. "He's sleeping and I didn't like to disturb him. He's got a hole in his head."

"Bad?" asked Hal anxiously.

"No; mere flesh wound. He'll be all right directly."

"And do you mean to tell me," demanded Hal, "that Ivan here did all this work?"

"Well, he did the greater part of it. It reminded me of the old days, when we watched Alexis in action. Any one who had ever seen them both fight would know they were brothers. Ivan is a powerful man and a great fighter."

Ivan had hung his head modestly as Chester talked. Now he looked up and said:

"It was nothing."

"And yet how unlike Alexis," muttered Hal. "Can you imagine what Alexis would have said after a fight like that?"

"Rather," said Chester dryly. "He'd have sworn he had defeated a regiment."

"Well," said Hal. "It seems to me we have delayed here long enough. You will remember your orders to hurry. My plane will carry us all, if Miss Ellison cares to go."

"Certainly she cares to go," returned Chester. "We can't leave her here alone. I'll wake Anderson now."

He did so. The Colonel announced that he was feeling perfectly fit and ready to go at any time.

"Well, you people get ready and I'll go and have a look at the plane," said Hal.

He left the house.

It had grown light by this time. Dawn had broken half an hour before and there was every indication that the day would be bright and cheerful.

Helen was upstairs getting her things together, while the others sat about in the parlor. Suddenly Hal dashed into the house. There was an expression of alarm on his face. The others jumped to their feet excitedly.

"Now what's the matter?" exclaimed Chester.

"Oh, nothing much," said Hal, "only that about fifty thousand Bulgarians have nabbed my aeroplane."

"What?" exclaimed the others.

"Exactly," said Hal, "and that's not the worst of it."

"My goodness!" exclaimed Stubbs. "What can be worse than that?"

"Well," replied Hal, sinking into a chair. "On the other side of us I made out about a million Serbians advancing."

"Great Scott!" exclaimed Chester. "You mean we are in

between them?"

"Precisely."

"Oh, my," groaned Stubbs. "This will be the last of us for sure."

"Quiet, Stubbs," said Hal sharply.

Now Ivan had a remark to make.

"There don't happen to be a million Serbians," he said calmly.

"Well, I wasn't talking literally," said Hal. "I don't know how many there are, but they look like a million."

"And what are we going to do?" moaned Stubbs.

"It looks to me as though we should have to stop right here," said Hal quietly.

"And be shot to pieces?" This from Stubbs.

"You might go outside and try running a bit," returned Chester. "I have no doubt you would be killed a bit quicker."

"I'll stay here," said Stubbs.

At this moment Helen came into the room. She was heavily attired and carried a small satchel.

"Well, I'm ready," she said, smiling. "Did you think it would take me all day to dress?"

"You might just as well go back and get unready," said

Stubbs in a faint voice.

Helen gazed at the serious faces about her queerly.

"Why, what on earth is the matter?" she asked anxiously.

"Matter?" echoed Stubbs. "Everything is the matter. The Serbians and Bulgarians are coming to shoot us full of holes."

Helen turned to Hal for an explanation.

"It's true, Miss Ellison, though not as Mr. Stubbs expresses it," said Hal quietly. "We are between two fires. The Bulgarians are less than half a mile from us and they have seized my airplane. The Serbians are advancing. There will undoubtedly be a battle and we will be somewhere about the middle of it."

"But can't we leave now and hurry toward the Serbians?" asked Helen.

"I had thought of that," said Hal; "but the Bulgarians are too close. If they saw us fleeing, they would probably shoot us down."

"Then cannot we seek the protection of the Bulgarians?"

This brought a growl from Ivan.

"Better keep as far from the Bulgarians as possible," he said in a harsh voice. "I know something of the Bulgarians."

Hal nodded.

"Besides, we have other business," he added. "We do not want to fall into the hands of the Bulgarians if we can

Clair W. Hayes

possibly help it. We have a mission to perform if it is humanly possible."

"Boom!" it was the sound of a big gun.

"The battle is on," said Hal. "Will any of you come to the roof with me? We should be able to get a good view."

"Boom! Boom! Boom! Boom! Boom!"

The battle was on in full blast.

CHAPTER XXVI

IN GRAVE PERIL

Helen led the way to the roof, the others following closely. As Hal had predicted, it was possible from this height to obtain a fair view of the opposing armies.

To the north, as far as the eye could see, the army of King Ferdinand of Bulgaria spread out, a mass of moving energy. Faint puffs of smoke dotted the Bulgar line as far as the eye could see.

"Cannon!" said Hal briefly.

To the south, the Serbian line moved forward. It, too, spread out on either side as far as the eye could reach and puffs of smoke rose steadily, shutting out the view of the moving men.

"More cannon," said Chester.

"We seem to be safe enough for the moment," said Hal. "The shells are passing over us. But if one side or the other should advance as far as this house, we would be in imminent danger of being struck by shells from the other side."

"Well, one side is bound to advance sooner or later," declared Chester; "but I guess there is nothing for us to do but wait and watch the progress of the battle."

"You fellows can watch all you want to," said Stubbs. "I'm going down stairs where I won't be able to see a shell coming."

"It won't make much difference whether you are up here or down there if a shell hits this house, Mr. Stubbs," said Chester.

"Maybe not; but I won't see it and that will help some."

Stubbs betook himself below.

"Don't know what is coming over Stubbs," said Chester. "He didn't use to be as bad as that."

"He was when we first met him," Hal replied. "But he seemed to be getting over it. He's worse than ever now."

From their position, those upon the roof of the house could witness the effect of some of the great shells that were hurled into the opposing lines. One, from the Serbians, struck squarely upon the Bulgarian first line troops, doing terrible execution. Men were mowed down in great numbers.

A few moments later the Bulgarians also found the range and the havoc was frightful on each side.

"They can't stand that very long," said Hal. "One side or the other will have to make a move."

The lad was right, and as it transpired the first move was to be made by the Serbians.

So suddenly that it appeared the work of magic, a great body of horsemen, stretching out for perhaps half a mile, issued from the Serbian line in a charge. On they came, their sabers flashing in the early morning sun, straight for the distant Bulgarian line.

Chester gave an exclamation of dismay.

"They'll pass within a short distance of us," he ejaculated. "Then the Bulgarians will turn their big guns on us." He turned to Helen. "You would better go downstairs, Miss Ellison," he said quietly.

"But I want to see the battle," the girl protested.

"Chester is right," Hal agreed. "This is no place for you. Bullets are likely to be flying about here before long now."

"But the rest of you are not coming down?"

"That's different," said Chester.

"I don't see how. A bullet is no more liable to hit me than it is to hit you."

"Well, of course if you insist, I won't push you down," said Hal, somewhat nettled.

Helen Ellison tossed her head.

"Of course if you are going to be mean about it, I'll go down and sit with Mr. Stubbs," she said.

Without another word she disappeared below.

Hal looked at Chester and smiled.

"Women and girls," he said, "are very peculiar. As soon as you agree with them they change their minds."

"Well, she's down, anyhow," said Chester. "That's some relief."

"And here come the Serbians," said Hal.

A handsome body of men, these Serbian cavalrymen, as they charged straight across the open field into the very jaws of death. Men fell on all sides, but those who were left did not pause. The command had gone forth that the Bulgarian guns must be silenced and the Serbians went about the work as coolly as though they had been on dress parade.

But it appeared a few moments later that the battle was not to be between horsemen and artillery, but rather between cavalry and cavalry.

From the Bulgarian lines now issued a large body of horsemen; and they came toward the Serbians at a swift gallop, their officers riding in front with swords flashing and urging their men on with words of encouragement.

The Serbian cavalry, at a command, halted and braced to receive the shock.

"Great Scott! What did they stop for!" exclaimed Hal. "They are giving the other fellows, all the advantage when they come together."

"Looks like bad generalship to me," Chester agreed.

Now, at a command from their officer, the Serbians resumed their charge; but the damage had been done and when the long lines of opposing horsemen came together the very impetus of the Bulgarian charge carried them through. The Serbians reeled, staggered and their line broke.

The Bulgarian horse plowed in among them, cutting, slashing and stabbing. Individually, the Serbians fought as bravely as their foe, but in spite of the desperate work the Bulgarian cavalry retained its cohesion and pushed steadily on.

The fighting was terrible to behold. Revolvers were brought into play and their sharp crack, crack could be heard above the sound of the trampling horses and yelling men. It became apparent to the onlookers that the Serbians were getting the worst of the encounter.

Casting his eye toward the main Serbian line, Hal gave a short cheer. A long, dense line of infantry was moving out to the support of the cavalry. Slowly they came at first, then faster and still faster as the men broke into a run. An imposing sight, indeed, and one to stir the blood. The Serbian cavalry, at a command, fell back upon the infantry, which separated into two sections to permit of the cavalry passing through the center. Then the infantry closed in again.

But the Bulgarian cavalry, with victory apparently within its grasp, had no intention of giving up now. With utter recklessness they charged the Serbian infantry, dying bravely before the rifles and upon the bayonets of their enemy when they chanced to escape the rifle fire.

The Serbian line held like a stone wall.

Then the Bulgarian cavalry drew off. A cheer, which arose from the Serbian line, was quickly checked as the giant batteries of the Bulgarians opened upon the unprotected Serbian line. The Serbians wavered, broke and fled.

Clair W. Hayes

Then once more the Bulgarian cavalry wheeled and charged. Right into the dense masses of Serbians rode the troopers, cutting and slashing to right and left. The execution among the panic-stricken Serbians was terrible to behold.

"They can't stand it long," Hal shouted, barely making himself heard above the roar of battle.

"The day is lost already," Chester shouted back.

There seemed no doubt of that now.

What was left of the Serbian infantry staggered back to the main army shattered and beaten. The big guns took up the battle again, but not with the same vigor and confidence as before. The Serbian fire seemed even to tell the spectators on the housetop that the Serbians had lost hope.

Half an hour later a general retreat began.

"Bad generalship, that's all," declared Hal.

"Without doubt," agreed Colonel Anderson. "A charge is a charge and once begun must be finished. That was where the Bulgarians gained the whip hand."

"The next step, I suppose, is an advance by the Bulgarians," said Chester.

"Very likely," Hal agreed, "and that means that we shall be caught in the Bulgarian lines."

"It means worse than that," said Colonel Anderson. "We are all in civilian attire and if our identities are discovered, it means that we'll be stood up and shot."

"By Jove!" said Hal. "I hadn't thought of that."

"Oh, we've been in predicaments just as serious," said Chester, "and we have always come through somehow. I guess we shall do so again."

"We'll get into one just once too often, I'm afraid," said Hal, "and this is likely to be it."

"You're getting as bad as Stubbs, Hal," said Chester. "Just keep a stiff upper lip and we'll come through this thing some way."

"I'm no quitter," said Hal. "But the best we can do now is let events shape themselves."

And now the Bulgarian advance began.

Apparently the Bulgarian commander had no thought of attempting to overtake the Serbians and annihilate them. Apparently he figured that ground gained was ground gained whether with or without a fight. The army moved forward slowly.

A party of officers, following in the wake of the vanguard, rode suddenly toward the house in which the friends had taken refuge.

"And here comes the trouble, as Stubbs would say," declared Hal. "Let's go below and get ready to receive them."

He suited the action to the word and the others followed him silently. Below, Hal acquainted Helen with what had transpired and announced that the Bulgarians were approaching.

"And what of the bodies without?" asked the girl quietly.

Clair W. Hayes

"Whew!" Hal gave a long and expressive whistle. "I hadn't thought of that. Wait a moment, though. We'll have to say they were here when the Serbians advanced and were killed."

"But the Serbians were not so close to the house."

"I know that, but I cannot think of any better excuse."

"Besides," said Stubbs, "if the Bulgarians were killed here by the Serbians, the chances are the Bulgarian commander will want to know how it happens we weren't killed also."

"Stubbs," said Hal, "I told you you were always a kill-joy. You can pick more flaws in things than any one I can think of. We'll tell the Bulgarians that story and take a chance on its passing muster."

"Then we may as well say our prayers now," said Stubbs mournfully.

"But what will we tell them we are?" asked Chester.

"Americans," replied Hal. "Caught here by the retreat. We were just making our way out of the country. I'll do the talking."

"All right," said Chester, and added: "Sh-h-h, here they come now!"

CHAPTER XXVII

PRISONERS

Came a knock at the door.

"You answer it, Miss Ellison, please," said Hal, adding: "If you are questioned, tell the same story you told Chester."

The girl nodded and moved to the door without a sign of nervousness. Directly she could be heard in conversation with one of the officers. Then followed heavy footsteps approaching.

"You say they are in here? I'll have a look at them myself," said a voice.

A moment later the scowling face of a Bulgarian colonel appeared in the doorway. Helen stood just behind him and behind her were several other Bulgarian officers.

Hal rose, as did the others, as the Bulgarian swept into the room.

"Who are you?" demanded the officer in a harsh voice.

"Hal Paine, an American," replied the lad, and indicated the others after this fashion: "Chester Crawford, also an American; Harry Anderson, an American; Nikol, an Albanian, the servant there of Anthony Stubbs, American war correspondent; Ivan Vergoff, also an Albanian."

"Hm-m-m," muttered the Bulgarian. "You have quite a fluent tongue, young man. And what are you doing here?"

"Three of us," said Hal, indicating Chester, Colonel Anderson and himself, "were looking about Montenegro when the war broke out. We have been there since, lending what aid we could to the wounded. There we encountered Ivan Vergoff, who, for some reason, became attached to us. There also we encountered Anthony Stubbs, war correspondent, and his man, Nikol. '

"Very plausible, very plausible," said the Bulgarian. "But how do I know you speak the truth?"

Hal shrugged his shoulders.

"We can't very well offer proof of our identities," he said. "But were the American consul here, I could very soon convince him."

The officer frowned at this remark. The mention of an American consul or minister or ambassador always brought frowns to the faces of military officers in the war zone. It boded trouble if American subjects were not well treated.

"And how do you happen to be here?" demanded the Bulgarian.

"Montenegro was becoming too warm," said Hal. "We thought we would get into Bulgaria or Greece, neutral countries. We did not know Bulgaria had declared war."

The Bulgarian's face seemed to relax a trifle. Apparently Hal had made a favorable impression.

"Well," he said, "the best I can do is turn you over to my superior. Still, if things are as you say, I have no doubt that you will be allowed to proceed into Greece."

"Thank you, Colonel," said Hal.

The officer glanced around the room; and suddenly his eyes fell upon a man lying in the corner of the room. It was the Bulgarian whom Ivan had tied up the night before.

"What's that?" demanded the officer.

He commanded another of his officers to investigate. Hal's heart fell.

The other officer stepped quickly across the room and jerked the man to his feet. Then he untied him and drew him before the Colonel. The latter, after one glance at the Bulgarian uniform, ordered his other men to guard all exits, and he addressed the man.

"What are you doing here, sir?" he asked sharply.

"I came here with some of my comrades last night," said the man. "I, a little in advance of the others, was overpowered and tied up. All I know of the others is that they arrived later and there was a fight. I have heard these people say my comrades were killed."

"Search the house and make a careful examination without!" ordered the Bulgarian officer.

Half a dozen of his men leaped to obey. The officer said

nothing until his men reported fifteen minutes later.

"The man speaks the truth," said one of the officers, indicating the Bulgarian.

The colonel whirled upon Hal.

"So," he exclaimed, "you have been lying to me. Perhaps you are not Americans, eh? Perhaps you are attached to the Anglo-French expedition at Saloniki?"

"I—" began Hal, but the officer silenced him with a gesture.

Then he turned to one of his officers.

"Take a squad of ten men and escort these prisoners to General Blozle!" he commanded shortly. "Search them for weapons first."

Hal and Chester realized the futility of resistance. They held their arms high, as did the others, and were relieved of their weapons without a word. Then, surrounded by a guard, they were marched away.

An hour later they stood before the Bulgarian commander, where the officer who had captured them related his story. General Blozle eyed them keenly.

"Have you anything to say?" he asked when the colonel had presented the case against them.

Chester stepped forward.

"Just this, general," he said quietly. "Miss Ellison here is in no way concerned in anything we may have done. We had never seen her until last night, as she told the colonel. Also, I would like to speak a word for Mr. Stubbs here. He is, as my friend has said, an American war correspondent. That's all, sir."

The lad resumed his place.

"Bah!" exclaimed the general. "You as much as admit you are a spy. If you are a spy, so are the others. You are a lot of spies. You English hounds! If it were not for the English, Bulgaria would now have what was rightfully hers. You shall all be shot at sunrise! Take them away!"

The prisoners were marched out with scant ceremony. They were taken to a large tent, with ample room for all of them. There they were securely bound and a guard stationed without.

"Well," said Stubbs quietly, with nothing of the fear of other days in his manner, "I guess we have come to the finish line at last."

"It looks that way, Mr. Stubbs," said Chester sadly. "I am sorry that we have implicated you in this."

"Oh, that's all right," replied the little man. "I'm not blaming you. But I would have liked to go back to New York once more."

Chester turned to Helen.

"And you, Miss Ellison," he said. "I hardly know what to say. If it had not been for me, you would not have been in this serious predicament."

Helen smiled at him.

Clair W. Hayes

"Say no more about it," she said quietly. "You saved me once. I am not the girl to whine now."

"Now that you people have all decided you are going to die, I would like to say a few words."

It was the voice of Nikol.

The others looked at him in surprise.

"What's the matter with you?" demanded Stubbs. "Want to berate us, I suppose, for getting you into this fix."

Nikol eyed Stubbs somewhat scornfully.

"I," said Nikol, "wish to say that while there is life there is hope."

"Good for you, old man," cried Hal. "You have expressed my thoughts exactly."

"Suppose you tell us how, securely tied as we are, we are going to get out of here?" Stubbs addressed Nikol.

"Very simple," said Nikol. "First I want to say this. I am no strategist. I can unloosen us all, if some one else will show us the way out."

"You do your part, Nikol, and I'll try and do mine," said Hal quietly.

The dwarf eyed him approvingly.

"You are the one person in the crowd who seems to have sense," he said. "As I say, I can break our bonds at any time. I can break the ropes that bind me and I have no doubt that

Ivan there can do the same."

Ivan nodded his head energetically.

"I had thought of it," he smiled. "Yes; I can do it."

"Then why haven't you done it a long while ago?" demanded Stubbs. "Anything is better than remaining here like this."

"I haven't done it before for fear of discovery," said Nikol.

"My idea exactly," agreed Ivan.

"It would be better," Nikol continued, "to wait until we are sure we shall not be disturbed again during the night. Then Ivan and I shall free ourselves and release the others. I believe it would be unwise now."

"Good reasoning, Nikol," said Hal. "We shall wait, as you suggest."

Nikol became silent again. Ivan said nothing either.

"But it's awfully tiresome being trussed up like this," Stubbs protested.

"Better a little tiresomeness now than a bullet in the morning, Mr. Stubbs," returned Chester.

"Right you are, Chester, I'll kick no more," said Stubbs.

He, too, became silent.

Hal, Chester and Colonel Anderson talked in low whispers.

"After we are freed of our bonds, then what?" questioned

the Colonel.

Chester shrugged his shoulders as much as his bonds would permit.

"Ask Hal," he replied. "I don't seem to be able to think of anything."

"Well," said Hal, "our guards, knowing that we are apparently securely bound, won't keep as strict guard as they should, I hope. Once freed, perhaps we can tap one of them over the head and appropriate his uniform. After that another uniform and so on until there are garments for all. We'll climb into them. Then we'll crawl under the tent, and once outside, we'll strike out boldly."

"And after that?" questioned Chester.

This time it was Hal who shrugged his shoulders.

"Who knows?" he said quietly. "We'll have to leave something to chance."

"And Miss Ellison?"

"A uniform for her also," said Hal decisively. "It's the only way."

"But—"

"Oh, I know it is a desperate chance," exclaimed Hal. "But certainly it is better than sitting down and awaiting the arrival of the firing squad."

"You're right, Hal," said Chester. "But it's a ticklish business and one that will require nerve."

"It's not a question of nerve, when you know what's in store in the morning," said Hal. "But as this is my plan, I'll do the work, or what part of it I may."

"You're the doctor," Chester agreed.

"Now," said Hal, "we'll try and get a little sleep. We can do nothing until after dark, and the better our physical conditions, the better our chances for escape."

CHAPTER XXVIII

THROUGH THE NIGHT

Hal, Chester, Colonel Anderson, Nikol and Ivan slept. The first three, veterans of many campaigns and hardships, had schooled themselves to sleep under almost any conditions. The same might be said of Nikol and Ivan because of days spent in the mountain fastness, where danger lurked at all times.

Stubbs, however, although he bore up bravely under the death sentence, was unable to sleep, try as he would. Nor could Helen gain a much needed rest, though she was not conscious that she was at all afraid. So these two talked during the long hours of the day as the others slept peacefully and deeply.

With the coming of darkness a man entered bearing a tray with bread and water. The others awakened now and all did full justice to the frugal meal. Their hands were untied while they ate, but the meal over, they were bound again.

Then all waited for what seemed hours, though in reality it could not have been more than three. Then Hal addressed Nikol.

"Still think you can break your bonds?"

"I can," replied Nikol quietly.

"And you, Ivan?"

"Yes, although it won't make much difference. Nikol could release the rest of us."

"I thought the second tying-up might have made it impossible," said Hal.

"I'm ready any time you give the word," said Nikol.

"Then do it now," said Hal.

The others gazed curiously as Nikol made his little form still smaller. He drew in his chest as much as possible and then expanded suddenly, at the same time thrusting out with his strong arms. There was a report as of a revolver being discharged, though much fainter, and Nikol was free.

"Ha!" said Ivan. "He did it. Now watch me."

The mighty muscles of the giant strained once and the strong rope snapped. Ivan did not seem to have exerted himself.

"Now for the rest of us," said Hal.

Quickly Ivan and Nikol released the others.

"Now what?" asked Ivan.

"Now comes my work," said Hal quietly.

He moved silently to the edge of the tent and lay down flat, feeling the edges with his fingers.

"This will come up all right," he muttered to himself. "I can get out here."

He went back to the center of the tent again and enjoined the others to silence.

"Don't make a sound on your lives," he commanded sternly. "Chester, you remain right where I leave the tent and if I bring a man back with me you drag him under and see that he doesn't make a sound.'

Chester nodded his agreement and took his place at Hal's side.

Now the lad lifted the bottom of the canvas slightly and peered out. He smiled a trifle to himself. It was as he hoped. The guard or guards, as the case might be, was not as vigilant as the security of the prisoners should have required. Hal wriggled into the open.

The huge camp slept. Here and there a sentinel stalked and it was upon these guardians of the night that Hal must prey.

He moved toward the front of the prison tent, seeking the guard there. And directly he came upon him, stretched at full length upon the ground, his heavy military coat pulled closely about him, smoking a cigarette. Hal moved toward him cautiously.

"I hate to do this," he muttered, "but—"

With a light leap he was upon the man and his right fist shot out hard and true. It caught the Bulgarian just above the left ear and the man never made a sound.

Quickly Hal dragged the body to where he knew Chester would be waiting. Chester dragged it under the tent and Hal went under after it.

"This uniform is for me. I'll go after some more," he said.

Quickly he climbed into the Bulgarian uniform and disappeared again. But this time, garbed in a Bulgarian uniform, he went more confidently. His hand rested upon his revolver.

A short distance away he came upon an unsuspecting sentinel. A sharp blow with his revolver butt placed the other *hors de combat*. Supporting the unconscious figure with his arm, Hal moved back to the prison tent. This figure also was pushed beneath the canvas and the uniform donned by Chester.

"Now we can make a little better time," said Hal, "there are two of us."

Uniforms were still needed for Colonel Anderson, Ivan, Nikol, Stubbs and Helen. Hal and Chester disappeared into the night.

Five minutes later Hal returned, this time with a uniform and no man. He had found him in a deserted spot, and after knocking him down and tying him up, had stripped him.

"Put this on, Anderson, and get out after one," he ordered.

He was gone again a moment later. Soon also Chester returned successful and he and Anderson departed almost together. There were now needed uniforms for Nikol, Stubbs and Helen, for Chester had brought one for Ivan. And these uniforms must necessarily be small uniforms, for they were for small figures. Therefore, the hunt was longer and it was more than an hour later until all three had returned to the tent.

"Well, here we are, all of us first class Bulgarians, now," said Hal. "Now, we'll leave the tent one at a time, except that I shall take Miss Ellison with me first. Now do exactly what I tell you, all of you. Leaving the tent, walk two hundred paces to the left, then turn to the right and walk a hundred and fifty more. Next fifty paces to the left again. We shall wait for you there. I have covered the distance and it's the best place to join forces I can imagine. It is in the shelter of a great rock that overhangs a large tent—probably the quarters of the commanding officer. Do you all understand?"

He had each repeat the directions several times, and then, taking Helen by the arm, he helped her under the tent.

Outside, with caps drawn down, for the weather was cold, they hurried on. And at the appointed place Hal stopped. There was nothing to do now but wait for the others.

Stubbs was the next to arrive and he came shaking a trifle. The little man was trying to bear up, but he was having a hard time. The next arrival was Nikol and then came Ivan. Chester was next to arrive, following Colonel Anderson by a few seconds.

"Now we're all here," said Hal. "We may as well move. I have no idea just where we are, so we'll have to select a direction and stick to it."

"Wait a moment, please," said Helen. "Isn't that the house in which we were captured?"

She pointed in the darkness. The others peered intently in the direction indicated. A dark shadow loomed up some distance ahead.

"I believe it is," said Hal. "Why?"

"Then, if you want to get into Greece, the quickest way is to go due south."

"But the question is, which is south?" said Hal.

"Oh, I can tell you that. You just follow the road that leads by the house."

"So be it," said Hal. "March."

With Chester and Helen he led the way.

They were forced to go very slowly for they were still in the Bulgarian lines, and all knew they would be for a considerable distance. How far the Bulgarians had extended their lines following the retreat of the Serbians they had of course no means of knowing, but Hal felt sure it would be a good ways.

Tents dotted their line of march for an hour as they walked along keeping parallel with the road, but some distance from the highway.

"This road will eventually lead across the Greek border," the girl whispered as they walked along.

"Here's hoping we get across the border before the Bulgarians get after us," said Chester.

"Second that motion," declared Hal.

They walked on in silence.

Clair W. Hayes

It had been more than an hour now since they had left their late prison and Hal was beginning to hope their absence would not be noticed before morning. He had just said as much to Chester.

"I am afraid that is too much to hope for," was the latter's reply.

And, as it turned out, it was.

The party had walked possibly five miles, when, from behind, they heard the sudden booming of a great gun.

"Faster," said Hal, and broke into a trot. The others followed suit.

"Suppose they have discovered our flight, or the gun was some other signal?" said Chester.

"I don't know," said Hal. "It's as likely to be one as the other. The farther away we get the better."

More guns now shattered the stillness of the night, growing closer and closer.

"They are after us, all right," declared Hal.

Without pausing, he glanced quickly around. Then suddenly he swerved sharply to the left.

"Why this change in course?" panted Chester.

"See that woods?" demanded Hal, pointing.

"Yes."

"Well, we may find safety there. It's a long chance."

They dashed into the shelter of the little woods a moment later.

Hal stopped and turned to Helen.

"Climb?" he asked.

"Why, yes, I guess so."

"Up in this tree with you then."

He lent her a hand as she grasped the lowest branch and soon clambered higher up toward the top.

"You too, Stubbs," he commanded.

The little man did not hesitate, but also was soon among the branches.

"Colonel Anderson, you and Nikol get up there also. I want some protection for Miss Ellison in case of trouble."

The others obeyed orders without question.

"All right," from each, and they moved toward him.

"Ivan, you come with me. You too, Chester."

Hal turned for a moment, to deliver a parting injunction to those in the trees:

"Don't any of you so much as move until I tell you to."

"And where are we bound?" asked Chester, as the three

moved off.

"Apparently," said Hal, "we are Bulgarian officers. The bluff may work. I want to tell all inquiring parties that we have just explored these woods. Catch the idea?"

Chester and Ivan nodded.

CHAPTER XXIX

MR. STUBBS PROVES HIMSELF

"We'll stay in among the trees and won't show ourselves unless we have to," Hal explained.

From the direction in which the fugitives had so recently come, there now came the noise of a rapidly approaching body of horsemen. They halted a short distance from where Hal, Chester and Ivan stood and dismounted.

"They may be hiding in here," said a voice. "We'll have a look."

The men, a dozen of them, came forward.

Making a slight detour, the three friends managed to get behind them. Then, instead of continuing straight ahead, Hal turned sharply in his tracks and followed in the wake of the Bulgarian searching party.

The Bulgarians proceeded slowly, exploring every nook and corner of the woods, and firing their rifles into the densest of the trees. Hal, Chester and Ivan came up with them at length and mingled among them without being discovered.

Clair W. Hayes

"Off to the left farther," instructed the officer in command.

"No use," said Hal, in a gruff voice. "I've just come from there. There is no one there. The fugitives must have gone farther."

"Are you sure?" asked the officer, looking at the lad searchingly.

"Positive. I fired my revolver into every tree in which I thought there was a possible chance for them to hide."

"There is no use wasting more time, then," said the officer. "This way, men."

He led the way back toward the road. Hal, Chester and Ivan, still among the Bulgarian troopers, were forced to go along with them or run the risk of being detected. They all walked slowly and gradually were left behind.

The Bulgarians mounted and rode off down the road.

"Well, we are safe for a few minutes," said Chester, drawing a breath of relief. "What now, Hal?"

"Well," was the reply. "We can't fool about in these woods long. We are bound to be found sooner or later if we do. Also, there is little chance that we could walk to the Greek frontier without being discovered. In some way we must find a conveyance."

"Yes, but how?" questioned Chester.

"That's the question. But certainly some of these Bulgarian officers must have motor cars. Surely they have some means of transportation besides horses. I have an idea that if we will follow them, in their search, we may come across an automobile."

"That's not a half bad idea," declared Chester. "We'll do it. Shall we start now?"

"Hold on," said Hal. "Either you or I must remain here. We can't both go. One of us has to direct the actions of the others."

"True," said Chester. "Will you go or stay?"

"Whatever you say," said Hal.

"Then," said Chester, "we shall match to see who goes."

He produced a coin and Hal did likewise.

"If I match you, I go," said Hal. "If not, you go."

"Agreed!"

The two coins went spinning in the air and each lad caught his own as it descended and covered it with his hand.

"Tails," said Chester.

"Tails," said Hal. "I go."

"All right," said Chester. "Then I'll be moving back toward the others. Good luck, old man, and hurry back."

The two lads clasped hands and Chester turned on his heel and strode away.

"You shall go with me, Ivan," said Hal.

The big Cossack showed his pleasure.

"I was afraid I was going to be left behind," he said. "I thought you might need me."

"I hope I won't," said Hal, "but you never can tell, you know. Let's be moving."

Again he led the way to the road and the two set out briskly.

After half an hour's walk they came upon a party of sear-chers. An officer hailed them as they approached.

"Seen anything of the fugitives?" he demanded.

Hal shook his head negatively.

"Did you?" he asked.

"Not a sign. It's a mystery what can have happened to them. Colonel Roth is a short distance ahead. I heard him say he believed they were still in the main camp."

"That so?" replied Hal. "How is the colonel traveling? Automobile?"

"Of course. He's too dainty for any other kind of travel, you know."

"Well, we'll move on ahead a bit," said Hal.

They continued their journey.

Fifteen minutes later they came upon a large touring car in the road.

"Here is the thing we want," said Hal quietly. "Now if it were just turned around, I would take a chance and grab it. But by the time I turned in this narrow road, I'd have the whole Bulgarian army on me. We'll have to do a little figuring."

They continued on their way until they came up with Colonel Roth's searching party. As they approached, an idea suddenly came to Hal. He sought out the man he knew must be Colonel Roth by his haughty air and his stripes.

"Colonel," he said, saluting. "I know it would be a feather in your cap if you could land these fugitives, and I have come to show you where they are."

"What's that?" exclaimed the dapper little man.

"I said I've come to show you where they are," said Hal quietly. "All I ask for turning them over to you is a thousand German marks."

"H-m-m-m," muttered the colonel, eyeing the lad keenly. "Even if you can do what you say, the price is rather high. I'll give you five hundred."

Hal seemed to consider.

"All right," he said at length. "It's a bargain. Turn your car about and I'll take you to their hiding place at once."

"Very well."

The colonel stepped into his automobile, and, after a series of attempts, finally succeeded in turning it. Then to the others:

Clair W. Hayes

"Climb in," he said briefly.

Ivan climbed into the rear seat, while Hal took his place beside the Bulgarian.

"Straight ahead until I tell you to stop," the lad instructed.

The Bulgarian officer asked no questions.

A few minutes later the machine drew up in response to Hal's command. All dismounted.

"They are all back here a little ways," said Hal.

The Bulgarian officer followed Hal toward where the lad knew the others were in hiding. Under the tree where he had left Helen, Hal paused. Then he raised his voice a trifle and called aloud, at the same time drawing his revolver and presenting it squarely at the Bulgarian's head:

"Chester! Oh, Chester! You can all come down now."

In response to this hail, Chester, Helen, Mr. Stubbs and Nikol soon stood before them.

When Hal drew his revolver, the Bulgarian officer staggered back.

"A traitor, eh?" he exclaimed.

"Why, no," said Hal, and he removed his heavy cap.

The Bulgarian gave a long whistle and ejaculated: "One of the fugitives himself."

"So you know me?" said Hal. "Well, then you should know

me well enough to do as I say."

"What is it you want?" demanded the Bulgarian.

"Nothing very difficult," declared Hal. "First we want to borrow your automobile for a few hours."

"So?" exclaimed the Bulgarian. "Well, you can't have it."

"We'll see," said Hal quietly. "Here, Ivan! You guard this fellow, while I have a look at the car."

He examined the machine carefully.

"All right for a quick dash, I guess," he said finally, rising from his inspection. "All aboard!"

Every one obeyed, and soon all were seated in the car save Hal and Chester, who were to occupy the front seat. Hal also motioned the Bulgarian into the front seat.

"He may come in handy after awhile," he declared.

Everything in readiness at last, Hal and Chester climbed in and Hal took his place at the wheel.

"I'll do the chauffeuring," he said, with a smile. "I may have to do some talking later and I want to be running this animal, so I can know what to do without having to talk. Keep your eye on our friend, there, Chester."

"I'll hang on to him, all right," replied Chester grimly. "He'll not get away from me. Have no fear of that."

"All right," called Hal. "Everybody ready?"

He glanced around quickly.

"All ready," came in Colonel Anderson's voice.

The others nodded their assent and an instant later the machine darted southward at a rapid gait.

Two miles down the road, Hal was forced to stop by the presence in the road of a single man armed with a rifle, which he aimed straight at the car.

"What do you want?" demanded Hal, anxiously.

"You'll have to get out," was the man's reply. "I have orders to let no one pass."

Helen looked at Hal hopelessly and the lad was moved to action.

Gently he stirred the Colonel with his toe as he commanded under his breath:

"Speak for us or I'll put a bullet through you."

The officer did as commanded.

"Why are you barring our way?" he demanded in a harsh voice.

"Orders, sir," was the reply.

"Do you know who I am?"

"No, sir, and it will make no difference."

This conversation was put to an end in a sudden and

unexpected manner.

Anthony Stubbs rose in his place.

"Will you permit us to proceed?" he demanded.

The man in the road shook his head.

"All right," said Stubbs.

He climbed to the front seat, and before any one could realize what he was up to, sprang head-first at the Bulgarian.

Clair W. Hayes

CHAPTER XXX

"GREATER LOVE HATH NO MAN"

Stubbs' action was so entirely unexpected that for a moment the other occupants of the automobile were stunned. Then Hal and Chester leaped to their feet, as did Nikol, Ivan and Colonel Anderson.

"Little man's gone off his head," muttered Ivan, as he leaped from the car to go to Stubbs' assistance.

Stubbs, in his headlong leap, struck exactly where he had intended—right upon the Bulgarian's shoulders, and the force of the impact bore the man to the ground. Again, the action was so unexpected that the man did not have time to discharge his rifle.

As the soldier went to the ground beneath his weight, Stubbs' hands gripped him by the throat and he squeezed as hard as his weak muscles would permit.

But the Bulgarian had recovered himself now and hurled Stubbs to one side. He pulled himself to his feet, and with an angry growl, half raised his rifle.

It was at that moment that Ivan, quicker than the others,

seized the rifle in his two hands. He gave a quick twist and jerked the weapon from the hands of his opponent. The latter staggered back and his hand dropped to his belt. But before he could draw a revolver, Ivan had raised his newly won rifle and brought it down on the Bulgarian's head. The man dropped inert without a sound.

Then Ivan picked Stubbs up bodily, deposited him in the tonneau of the car and climbed in himself.

"We'd better get away from here," he said.

Quickly Hal resumed his seat and threw off the clutch. The automobile dashed forward again.

Ivan turned to Stubbs.

"Why all this bloodthirstiness, Mr. Stubbs?" he demanded in surprise.

"I'm getting tired of all this nonsense," replied Stubbs. "I want to get out of this country. I want to get back home where there is no war—where men are not killing each other off by the thousands. I'm a peaceable man and I'm going back to a peaceable country if I have to fight to get there."

Nikol the dwarf now extended a hand to Stubbs.

"You are a brave man, sir," he exclaimed. "Not many are there who would have attacked a man who held a rifle pointed at his breast. You are a brave man, sir."

Unthinkingly, Stubbs clasped the hand and a moment later gave a howl of pain.

"Hey! Leggo my hand!" he cried. "Ouch!"

Nikol released Stubbs' hand with a murmured apology, while Stubbs felt the injured right member tenderly with his left and turned an aggrieved eye on Nikol, but he said nothing.

Suddenly the car slowed down. Those in the rear seat glanced ahead and the reason for the abrupt slackening of speed became apparent.

Coming toward them at a rapid trot was a squadron of Bulgarian cavalry, blocking the road.

Hal turned to the Bulgarian officer between him and Chester and said quietly:

"Now it's up to you. Remember, I've got my gun ready and at the first false move I'll put a bullet through you."

The captain in command of the cavalry squadron gave a sharp command and his men drew rein while the officer came forward. He glanced at the colonel in the automobile and saluted.

"Oh, it's you, sir," he said. "Have you seen anything of the fugitives?"

The Bulgarian felt the pressure of Hal's revolver in his back.

"No," he said.

The captain saluted and would have passed on, but Hal instructed his prisoner to ask:

"How far are we from the Greek frontier?"

"Less than a mile," was the answer. "There is but one more body of our troops between here and a strong force of

Greeks, which is patrolling the border."

The two Bulgarians saluted each other and the troop separated to make a path for the automobile.

"Another close shave for all of us," said Chester, when they had passed by. "You, too," he said to the Bulgarian. "You'd have been a goner if you had sought to give the alarm."

A few minutes later Hal made out another body of troops blocking the road. He reduced the speed of the car and spoke to the others.

"The last barrier to freedom," he said. "Be ready to duck down in the car. I am going to take no more chances with our prisoner here. He is likely to take this last chance to betray us. The troops are drawn up on both sides of the road. I am going to make a dash for it."

There was no reply, but Hal had expected none.

The car approached the troops slowly and seemed about to stop.

The Bulgarians moved to one side, thinking to surround the machine when it had come to a halt.

Less than fifty feet from the nearest soldiers, and a scant two hundred yards from where Hal could make out a large body of Greek troops, the car suddenly leaped ahead and Hal threw the gear into high.

All save Hal ducked instinctively.

The Bulgarians, taken completely by surprise, stood stock still for a moment and then the cry of in officer rang out:

"Fire!"

Instantly fifty rifles were leveled at the automobile, now fast eating up the short distance to the Greek frontier, and a score of bullets struck the car in the rear.

Bullets flew all about Hal's head and he felt a stinging sensation in his left shoulder. There came a second volley and then the car flashed among the body of Greek troops.

Quickly Hal brought the car to a stop. Heads bobbed up from the back of the car and it was Anthony Stubbs who breathed the relief that all felt.

"Safe at last!" he cried.

Now all alighted from the car, the Bulgarian officer, Hal's prisoner, with them.

Greek troops approached.

Hal spoke hurriedly to the Bulgarian.

"Quick now!" he cried. "If you make a dash you can get back over the border before these fellows can stop you."

The Bulgarian wasted no time in talk. He took to his heels and made record time for his own country, which he reached in safety, in spite of a volley fired by the Greek troops.

A Greek officer now came hurriedly up to Hal.

"What is the meaning of this?" he demanded harshly. "Do you not know that this is a neutral country?"

"And we thank Heaven for that," said Stubbs fervently. "We

have had a hard enough time getting here."

"I shall have to turn you over to my superior," said the officer. "He will dispose of your cases. In the meantime, you may consider yourselves under arrest."

Neither Hal nor Chester paid much attention to what the Greek officer was saying. They were too busily engaged watching the antics of their erstwhile prisoner, who, now safe on his own side of the line, was shaking his fist in their direction and making other fierce gestures.

Now Hal turned to the Greek officer.

"Will you accompany us back close to the line," he said, "that we may hear what yonder little fellow is talking about? He seems to be greatly put out about something."

"First tell me what you are doing here?" was the command.

Hal explained as rapidly as possible and then repeated his request that they be allowed to go back toward the border a few moments.

At last the officer gave his permission.

Chester, Hal, Colonel Anderson, Ivan and Nikol, each grinning, moved back toward the border. Stubbs hung back, and seeing this, Hal called:

"Come along, Mr. Stubbs. Here is one time you may look at an enemy with impunity."

Stubbs followed.

The Bulgarian officer was still angrily waving hit arms about

Clair W. Hayes

when they neared him.

"Look at him rave, will you?" said Hal, with a laugh.

"Ha! Ha!" laughed Ivan.

"He should think himself lucky that we allowed him to go back," declared Chester.

The friends were less than fifty feet from the Bulgarian now, but they ventured no closer for fear they might inadvertently cross the line. They stood in this order: Hal, Chester, Nikol, Stubbs, Ivan and Colonel Anderson.

"Poor little fellow," said Stubbs at this juncture. "Poor little fellow. He looks so awfully mad!"

The Bulgarian officer, who had been growing angrier with each taunt from across the Greek line, now became suddenly infuriated. Forgetting all prudence, forgetting all laws of neutrality, forgetting everything except the smiling face of Anthony Stubbs, American war correspondent, he suddenly drew his revolver and fired pointblank at the little man.

Stubbs' face blanched at the movement and the others were too surprised to move—all except one; and this one, quick as a flash, leaped forward with the agility of a cat and thrust his body protectingly before Anthony Stubbs.

When the smoke of the revolver had cleared away Stubbs stood erect, unharmed—but at his feet lay the twitching body of Nikol, the dwarf.

There was a sudden hush, prolonged for several minutes; then Stubbs dropped to his knee with an inarticulate cry and threw his arms around the neck of Nikol.

Quickly the others gathered about and Hal shouted:

"A surgeon, quick!"

But Nikol, raising his head to Stubbs' knee, stopped him with a gesture.

"It's no use," he said quietly. "It got me here," and he raised a hand slowly and touched a spot just above the heart. "A surgeon can do no good. Besides, I would not have a stranger near me when I die. To me you are all strangers and yet for days I have not looked upon you as such. I am glad to have known you all and I know the day will come when I shall see you all again. Now, if I could see the young lady for just a moment before—before—"

Hal hastened back to the automobile where Helen Ellison still sat, wondering at the cause of the trouble, and repeated the dwarf's request.

"Of course I'll go," said the girl, and there was a catch in her voice, for this was the first time death had come so close to her.

She ran forward and knelt over the little dwarf and took his hand. He smiled at her.

"I just wanted to tell you good-bye," he said. "I have never seen a young lady like you before."

For a space of several seconds he looked at her. Then he dropped her hand and said:

"Now if the rest of you will just shake hands with me once—"

Silently the others grasped Nikol's hand, one after another,

Clair W. Hayes

and at the last came Stubbs.

To the latter's hand the dwarf clung tenaciously.

"You, sir, are a brave man." said Nikol. "I am glad I was able to save you. You may be of some use in the world."

The pressure upon Stubbs' hand tightened and tightened until the little man winced with the pain of it; but he made no outcry—only smiled as he exclaimed in a broken voice:

"Nonsense! Nonsense!"

"Well, good-bye, all," said Nikol faintly, after a moment's pause. "Good—"

The pressure on Stubbs' hand relaxed and the little dwarf of the Albanian hills fell back, dead.

Stubbs rose and brushed the tears from his eyes. Then, after one look at the still form on the ground, he turned and walked away. The others said nothing, for they knew his grief was great.

And now, while the others—all good friends and true—are gathered about the body of little Nikol, the dwarf, we shall leave them once more, knowing that, after days and weeks of strenuous adventures and grave perils, they are, for the moment at least, in a land of peace.

THE END

Choose from Thousands of 1stWorldLibrary Classics By

A. M. Barnard
Ada Leverson
Adolphus William Ward
Aesop
Agatha Christie
Alexander Aaronsohn
Alexander Kielland
Alexandre Dumas
Alfred Gatty
Alfred Ollivant
Alice Duer Miller
Alice Turner Curtis
Alice Dunbar
Allen Chapman
Alleyne Ireland
Ambrose Bierce
Amelia E. Barr
Amory H. Bradford
Andrew Lang
Andrew McFarland Davis
Andy Adams
Angela Brazil
Anna Alice Chapin
Anna Sewell
Annie Besant
Annie Hamilton Donnell
Annie Payson Call
Annie Roe Carr
Annonaymous
Anton Chekhov
Archibald Lee Fletcher
Arnold Bennett
Arthur C. Benson
Arthur Conan Doyle
Arthur M. Winfield
Arthur Ransome
Arthur Schnitzler
Arthur Train
Atticus
B.H. Baden-Powell
B. M. Bower
B. C. Chatterjee
Baroness Emmuska Orczy
Baroness Orczy
Basil King
Bayard Taylor
Ben Macomber
Bertha Muzzy Bower
Bjornstjerne Bjornson

Booth Tarkington
Boyd Cable
Bram Stoker
C. Collodi
C. E. Orr
C. M. Ingleby
Carolyn Wells
Catherine Parr Traill
Charles A. Eastman
Charles Amory Beach
Charles Dickens
Charles Dudley Warner
Charles Farrar Browne
Charles Ives
Charles Kingsley
Charles Klein
Charles Hanson Towne
Charles Lathrop Pack
Charles Romyn Dake
Charles Whibley
Charles Willing Beale
Charlotte M. Braeme
Charlotte M. Yonge
Charlotte Perkins Stetson
Clair W. Hayes
Clarence Day Jr.
Clarence E. Mulford
Clemence Housman
Confucius
Coningsby Dawson
Cornelis DeWitt Wilcox
Cyril Burleigh
D. H. Lawrence
Daniel Defoe
David Garnett
Dinah Craik
Don Carlos Janes
Donald Keyhoe
Dorothy Kilner
Dougan Clark
Douglas Fairbanks
E. Nesbit
E. P. Roe
E. Phillips Oppenheim
E. S. Brooks
Earl Barnes
Edgar Rice Burroughs
Edith Van Dyne
Edith Wharton

Edward Everett Hale
Edward J. O'Biren
Edward S. Ellis
Edwin L. Arnold
Eleanor Atkins
Eleanor Hallowell Abbott
Eliot Gregory
Elizabeth Gaskell
Elizabeth McCracken
Elizabeth Von Arnim
Ellem Key
Emerson Hough
Emilie F. Carlen
Emily Bronte
Emily Dickinson
Enid Bagnold
Enilor Macartney Lane
Erasmus W. Jones
Ernie Howard Pie
Ethel May Dell
Ethel Turner
Ethel Watts Mumford
Eugene Sue
Eugenie Foa
Eugene Wood
Eustace Hale Ball
Evelyn Everett-green
Everard Cotes
F. H. Cheley
F. J. Cross
F. Marion Crawford
Fannie E. Newberry
Federick Austin Ogg
Ferdinand Ossendowski
Fergus Hume
Florence A. Kilpatrick
Fremont B. Deering
Francis Bacon
Francis Darwin
Frances Hodgson Burnett
Frances Parkinson Keyes
Frank Gee Patchin
Frank Harris
Frank Jewett Mather
Frank L. Packard
Frank V. Webster
Frederic Stewart Isham
Frederick Trevor Hill
Frederick Winslow Taylor

Friedrich Kerst	Hayden Carruth	James Branch Cabell
Friedrich Nietzsche	Helent Hunt Jackson	James DeMille
Fyodor Dostoyevsky	Helen Nicolay	James Joyce
G.A. Henty	Hencrik Conscience	James Lane Allen
G.K. Chesterton	Hendy David Thoreau	James Lane Allen
Gabrielle E. Jackson	Henri Barbusse	James Oliver Curwood
Garrett P. Serviss	Henrik Ibsen	James Oppenheim
Gaston Leroux	Henry Adams	James Otis
George A. Warren	Henry Ford	James R. Driscoll
George Ade	Henry Frost	Jane Abbott
Geroge Bernard Shaw	Henry James	Jane Austen
George Cary Eggleston	Henry Jones Ford	Jane L. Stewart
George Durston	Henry Seton Merriman	Janet Aldridge
George Ebers	Henry W Longfellow	Jens Peter Jacobsen
George Eliot	Herbert A. Giles	Jerome K. Jerome
George Gissing	Herbert Carter	Jessie Graham Flower
George MacDonald	Herbert N. Casson	John Buchan
George Meredith	Herman Hesse	John Burroughs
George Orwell	Hildegard G. Frey	John Cournos
George Sylvester Viereck	Homer	John F. Kennedy
George Tucker	Honore De Balzac	John Gay
George W. Cable	Horace B. Day	John Glasworthy
George Wharton James	Horace Walpole	John Habberton
Gertrude Atherton	Horatio Alger Jr.	John Joy Bell
Gordon Casserly	Howard Pyle	John Kendrick Bangs
Grace E. King	Howard R. Garis	John Milton
Grace Gallatin	Hugh Lofting	John Philip Sousa
Grace Greenwood	Hugh Walpole	John Taintor Foote
Grant Allen	Humphry Ward	Jonas Lauritz Idemil Lie
Guillermo A. Sherwell	Ian Maclaren	Jonathan Swift
Gulielma Zollinger	Inez Haynes Gillmore	Joseph A. Altsheler
Gustav Flaubert	Irving Bacheller	Joseph Carey
H. A. Cody	Isabel Cecilia Williams	Joseph Conrad
H. B. Irving	Isabel Hornibrook	Joseph E. Badger Jr
H. C. Bailey	Israel Abrahams	Joseph Hergesheimer
H. G. Wells	Ivan Turgenev	Joseph Jacobs
H. H. Munro	J. G.Austin	Jules Vernes
H. Irving Hancock	J. Henri Fabre	Julian Hawthrone
H. R. Naylor	J. M. Barrie	Julie A Lippmann
H. Rider Haggard	J. M. Walsh	Justin Huntly McCarthy
H. W. C. Davis	J. Macdonald Oxley	Kakuzo Okakura
Haldeman Julius	J. R. Miller	Karle Wilson Baker
Hall Caine	J. S. Fletcher	Kate Chopin
Hamilton Wright Mabie	J. S. Knowles	Kenneth Grahame
Hans Christian Andersen	J. Storer Clouston	Kenneth McGaffey
Harold Avery	J. W. Duffield	Kate Langley Bosher
Harold McGrath	Jack London	Kate Langley Bosher
Harriet Beecher Stowe	Jacob Abbott	Katherine Cecil Thurston
Harry Castlemon	James Allen	Katherine Stokes
Harry Coghill	James Andrews	L. A. Abbot
Harry Houidini	James Baldwin	L. T. Meade

L. Frank Baum
Latta Griswold
Laura Dent Crane
Laura Lee Hope
Laurence Housman
Lawrence Beasley
Leo Tolstoy
Leonid Andreyev
Lewis Carroll
Lewis Sperry Chafer
Lilian Bell
Lloyd Osbourne
Louis Hughes
Louis Joseph Vance
Louis Tracy
Louisa May Alcott
Lucy Fitch Perkins
Lucy Maud Montgomery
Luther Benson
Lydia Miller Middleton ·
Lyndon Orr
M. Corvus
M. H. Adams
Margaret E. Sangster
Margret Howth
Margaret Vandercook
Margaret W. Hungerford
Margret Penrose
Maria Edgeworth
Maria Thompson Daviess
Mariano Azuela
Marion Polk Angellotti
Mark Overton
Mark Twain
Mary Austin
Mary Catherine Crowley
Mary Cole
Mary Hastings Bradley
Mary Roberts Rinehart
Mary Rowlandson
M. Wollstonecraft Shelley
Maud Lindsay
Max Beerbohm
Myra Kelly
Nathaniel Hawthrone
Nicolo Machiavelli
O. F. Walton
Oscar Wilde
Owen Johnson
P.G. Wodehouse
Paul and Mabel Thorne

Paul G. Tomlinson
Paul Severing
Percy Brebner
Percy Keese Fitzhugh
Peter B. Kyne
Plato
Quincy Allen
R. Derby Holmes
R. L. Stevenson
R. S. Ball
Rabindranath Tagore
Rahul Alvares
Ralph Bonehill
Ralph Henry Barbour
Ralph Victor
Ralph Waldo Emmerson
Rene Descartes
Ray Cummings
Rex Beach
Rex E. Beach
Richard Harding Davis
Richard Jefferies
Richard Le Gallienne
Robert Barr
Robert Frost
Robert Gordon Anderson
Robert L. Drake
Robert Lansing
Robert Lynd
Robert Michael Ballantyne
Robert W. Chambers
Rosa Nouchette Carey
Rudyard Kipling
Saint Augustine
Samuel B. Allison
Samuel Hopkins Adams
Sarah Bernhardt
Sarah C. Hallowell
Selma Lagerlof
Sherwood Anderson
Sigmund Freud
Standish O'Grady
Stanley Weyman
Stella Benson
Stella M. Francis
Stephen Crane
Stewart Edward White
Stijn Streuvels
Swami Abhedananda
Swami Parmananda
T. S. Ackland

T. S. Arthur
The Princess Der Ling
Thomas A. Janvier
Thomas A Kempis
Thomas Anderton
Thomas Bailey Aldrich
Thomas Bulfinch
Thomas De Quincey
Thomas Dixon
Thomas H. Huxley
Thomas Hardy
Thomas More
Thornton W. Burgess
U. S. Grant
Upton Sinclair
Valentine Williams
Various Authors
Vaughan Kester
Victor Appleton
Victor G. Durham
Victoria Cross
Virginia Woolf
Wadsworth Camp
Walter Camp
Walter Scott
Washington Irving
Wilbur Lawton
Wilkie Collins
Willa Cather
Willard F. Baker
William Dean Howells
William le Queux
W. Makepeace Thackeray
William W. Walter
William Shakespeare
Winston Churchill
Yei Theodora Ozaki
Yogi Ramacharaka
Young E. Allison
Zane Grey